Sous Vide Grilling

The Best Recipes and Techniques
for Using Your Grill
with Sous Vide Cooking

By Jason Logsdon

Part of the *Cooking Sous Vide* Series
Presented By CookingSousVide.com

For more information please contact Primolicious LLC at 12 Pimlico Road, Wolcott CT 06716.

Cover Photo Credit: http://www.flickr.com/photos/katerha

ISBN-13: 978-1461135371
ISBN-10: 1461135370

TABLE OF CONTENTS

SOUS VIDE BASICS   1
History of Sous Vide   2
How it Works   2
Basic Sous Vide Technique   3
Sous Vide Grilling   5
Sous Vide Safety   5

SOUS VIDE AT BBQ PARTIES   9
Cooking Party Foods   10
Benefits of Sous Vide   10
Tips and Tricks   10
Sample Party Food Menus   11

CONVERTING EXISTING RECIPES   13
Isolate Seasonings   14
Determine Time and Temperature   14
Choose Your Finishing Method   14
Putting it All Together   15

SOUS VIDE AND GRILLING TIPS   17
Flavor   18
Finishing   19
General Grilling   19
Adding Smoke   20

SALADS   21
Cooking Salads   22
Tips and Tricks   22

KEBABS   37
Cooking Kebabs   38
Tips and Tricks   38

BURGERS AND SANDWICHES   47
Cooking Burgers and Sandwiches   48
Tips and Tricks   48

SAUSAGES AND HOTDOGS   59
Cooking Sausages and Hotdogs   60
Tips and Tricks   60

CLASSIC BBQ   71
Cooking Classic BBQ   72
Tips and Tricks   72

BEEF STEAKS AND ROASTS   79
Cooking Beef Steaks and Roasts   80
Tips and Tricks   80

CHICKEN AND POULTRY   99
Cooking Chicken and Poultry   100
Tips and Tricks   100

FISH AND SHELLFISH   115
Cooking Fish and Shellfish   116
Tips and Tricks   116

LAMB   125
Cooking Lamb   126
Tips and Tricks   126

PORK   135
Cooking Pork   136
Tips and Tricks   136

TIME AND TEMPERATURE CHARTS 143

Doneness Range	144
Beef Roasts and Tough Cuts	146
Beef - Steak and Tender Cuts	147
Chicken and Eggs	148
Duck	149
Fish and Shellfish	150
Fruits and Vegetables	153
Lamb	154
Pork	155
Turkey	157
Fahrenheit to Celsius Conversion	158

COOKING BY THICKNESS 159

Beef, Pork, Lamb Thickness Chart	161
Chicken Thickness Chart	163
Fish Thickness Chart	165

SOUS VIDE RESOURCES 167

Books	168
Websites	169
Papers and Research	170
Photo Credits	171

SOUS VIDE BASICS

For a more detailed look at sous vide, the equipment needed, and the specifics of the process you can view our free Beginning Sous Vide guide on our website.

You can find them on our website at:
www.cookingsousvide.com/beginning-sous-vide-guide.html

HISTORY OF SOUS VIDE

Sous vide, or low temperature cooking, is the process of cooking food at a very tightly controlled temperature, normally the temperature the food will be served at. This is a departure from traditional cooking methods that use high heat to cook the food, which must be removed at the exact moment it reaches the desired temperature.

Sous vide was first used as an upscale culinary technique in kitchens in France in the 1970s and traditionally is the process of cooking vacuum sealed food in a low temperature water bath. This process helps to achieve texture and doneness not found in other cooking techniques, as well as introducing many conveniences for a professional kitchen. Sous vide has slowly been spreading around the world in professional kitchens everywhere and is finally making the jump to home kitchens.

As sous vide has become more popular and moved to the home kitchen the term now encompasses both traditional "under vacuum" sous vide and also low temperature cooking. Some preparations rely on the vacuum pressure to change the texture of the food but in most cases the benefits of sous vide are realized in the controlled, low temperature cooking process. This means that fancy vacuum sealers can be set aside for home sealers or even ziploc bags.

HOW IT WORKS

The basic concept of sous vide cooking is that food should be cooked at the temperature it will be served at. For instance, if you are cooking a steak to medium rare, you want to serve it at 131°F.

With traditional cooking methods you would normally cook it on a hot grill or oven at around 400°F-500°F and pull it off at the right moment when the middle has reached 131°F. This results in a bulls eye effect of burnt meat on the outside turning to medium rare in the middle. This steak cooked sous vide would be cooked at 131°F for several hours. This will result in the entire piece of meat being a perfectly cooked medium rare. The steak would then usually be quickly seared at high heat to add the flavorful, browned crust to it.

There are two basic components to sous vide cooking at home: temperature and time. Each one of these can affect the end quality, texture, and taste of sous vide dishes. Learning to understand how they affect the food is one of the most important things as you begin sous vide cooking.

Temperature

All sous vide cooking is done at temperatures below the boiling point of water and normally not above 185°F. You usually cook the food at the temperature you want it served at, so most settings are between 120°F and 185°F, depending on the food being prepared.

While the range of temperature used in sous vide is much less variable than for traditional cooking, the precise control of the temperature is of great importance. When you set your oven at 400°F it actually fluctuates about 50 degrees, sending it between 375°F and 425°F, which is fine when cooking at high temperatures. When cooking sous vide, the temperature of the water determines the doneness of your food, so a 50°F fluctuation would result in over-cooked food. Most sous vide machines fluctuate less than 1°F and the best are less than 0.1°F.

This precision is why many sous vide machines are very expensive. However, there are many more home machines available in the last few years, some good do-it-yourself kits, and even some ways to accomplish "accurate enough" sous vide on the cheap. We discuss many of your options in our free online Beginning Sous Vide Guide (http://bit.ly/e8MvOu).

Time

Cooking tenderizes food by breaking down its internal structure. This process happens faster at higher temperatures. Because sous vide is done at such low temperatures the cooking time needs to be increased to achieve the same tenderization as traditional techniques.

Also, your window of time to perfectly cooked food is much longer than with traditional cooking methods because you are cooking the food at the temperature you want it to end up at, rather than a higher temperature. This also allows you to leave food in the water bath even after it is done since keeping it at this temperature does not dry out the food, up to several hours longer for tougher cuts of meat. However, be careful not to take this concept too far as food can still become overcooked by sous vide, many times without showing it externally.

Temperature and Time Together

The power of sous vide cooking comes from precisely controlling both temperature and time. This is important because of the way meat reacts to different temperatures.

At 120°F meat slowly begins to tenderize as the protein myosin begins to coagulate and the connective tissue in the meat begins to break down. As the temperature increases so does the speed of tenderization.

However, meat also begins to lose its moisture above 140°F as the heat causes the collagen in the cells to shrink and wring out the moisture. This happens very quickly over 150°F and meat becomes completely dried out above 160°F.

Many tough cuts of meat are braised or roasted for a long period of time so the meat can fully tenderize, but because of the high temperatures they can easily become dried out. Using sous vide allows you to hold the meat below the 140°F barrier long enough for the slower tenderization process to be effective. This results in very tender meat that is still moist and not overcooked.

BASIC SOUS VIDE TECHNIQUE

At the heart of sous vide cooking is a very simple process. While there are variations within each dish, almost every sous vide meal follows the same steps.

Flavor the Food

Just like many traditional methods, you often times flavor the food before cooking it. This can be as simple as a sprinkling of salt and pepper or as complicated as adding an elaborate sauce, spice rub, or even smoking the food. Depending on the type of seasoning it can either be rubbed directly onto the food itself or added into the pouch with the food.

If you are using a normal home vacuum sealer and want to add more than a little liquid, freeze the liquid before adding it to the pouch. This way the process of vacuum sealing will not suck out the liquid. Otherwise, you can normally use food grade ziploc bags to seal food with liquids.

In our various food sections we give some tips and suggested recipes for flavoring your food. But remember, just like traditional cooking a lot of the fun comes with experimenting.

Seal the Food

Once the seasoning and food have been added to the pouch, remove the air and seal it closed. Removing the air results in closer contact between the food and the water in the water bath. This helps to facilitate quicker cooking since water transfers heat more efficiently than air.

Sealing the food can be done with anything from ziplocs or food grade plastic wrap to a FoodSaver Vacuum Sealer or even a chambered vacuum sealer. We discuss many of your options in our free online Beginning Sous Vide Guide (http://bit.ly/e8MvOu)

Some vacuum sealers have different strengths of vacuum to seal the bag and can be used to affect the texture of some types of food.

If you are using ziploc bags to seal your food you can use this trick to force out the majority of the air. Once the bag is ready to close, seal the bag except for 1" of it. Place the bag into the water bath making sure to keep that last 1" out of the water. The water will force the remaining air out of the bag and then you can seal it completely. When done properly this is almost as good as using a weak vacuum sealer and will work great for most low-temperature sous vide cooking.

Heat the Water

Simply bring the water bath up to the temperature you will cook at. This water bath will normally be the same temperature that you will want your food to end up at.

Depending on the type of heat regulator, you may be able to have the food in the water while it heats. For others, it is best to preheat the water before placing the food in it due to early fluctuations in temperature.

You can use anything from a pot on a stove to a beer cooler to a professional immersion circulator. We discuss many of your options in our free online Beginning Sous Vide Guide (http://bit.ly/e8MvOu)

Cook the Food

Put the food pouch in the water and let it cook for the amount of time specified in the recipe or on the Time and Temperature chart. For items that are cooked for longer amounts of time it can be good to rotate the food every 6 to 10 hours, especially if you are using less precise sous vide equipment.

At some higher temperatures the sous vide pouches can float due to air released from the food. If that happens you might have to use a plate or bowl to weight them down.

If you are unfamiliar with how sous vide cooking times work please read our Doneness Range section in the Time and Temperature Chart chapter.

Finish the Dish

To get a good finish and texture to your food, especially meats, it is usually advisable to quickly sear the meat. In this book we focus on using the grill to finish off dishes but you can also use a hot pan or a culinary blow torch. Some meals also call for other methods of finishing the food, such as breading and deep-frying for chicken or mashing potatoes with cream and butter for mashed potatoes.

You can also quickly chill the food in an ice bath which is ½ ice and ½ water and then refrigerate or freeze the food for later re-heating.

Sous Vide Grilling

Sous vide adds a lot of convenience to many different types of cooking. One of the areas this is very apparent is for grilling meats or cooking BBQ. You can use sous vide to free up a lot of time that you would usually spend hovering around the grill.

There are a few different ways to utilize sous vide for grilling and BBQ. And if you are one of those people (like me) who loves to hang out by the grill, you can still do that while utilizing sous vide, you're just doing it because you *want* to, not because you *have* to.

There are two main ways to apply sous vide cooking to grilling and BBQ.

Cook and Hold

The first way to utilize sous vide is to cook your food sous vide and have it timed so it will enter the Doneness Range when you will want to start serving people. You just hold your food in the water bath until you are ready to eat it then you remove what you need, pat it dry, and quickly sear it.

Most foods have a large Doneness Range and you can utilize this to hold the food until you're ready to eat.

Cook and Chill

The second main way to use sous vide is to cook your food (often a day or two before) and then quickly chill it in a ½ ice ½ water bath. You then bring it back up to temperature around the time you're ready to eat and then quickly grill it.

This is a great method if you are serving many different kinds of food that need to be cooked at different temperatures. You can cook each one separately, chill them, and put them in the refrigerator until you are ready to eat.

It is also a great way to prepare many meals ahead of time, like during a busy work week. Simply cook the food ahead of time, quick chill it, and put it in the refrigerator. Then during the week, once you get home from work you can pull out the food and quickly grill it just long enough to develop great grill marks and also bring the center up to temperature.

Sous Vide Safety

Sous vide is a new and largely untested method of cooking. It potentially carries many inherent health risks that may not be fully understood. We have done our best to provide the latest information and what is currently understood about this form of cooking.

However, we feel that anyone undertaking sous vide cooking, or any other method of cooking, should fully inform themselves about any and all risks associated with it and come to their own conclusions about its safety. Following anything in this book may make you or your guests sick and should only be done if you are fully aware of the potential risks and complications.

There are two main concerns when it comes to sous vide cooking, they are pathogens and the dangers of cooking in plastic.

Pathogens, Bacteria and Salmonella

One large safety concern with sous vide that has been studied in great detail deals with the propagation of bacteria at various temperatures, especially salmonella. Salmonella only thrive in a certain range of temperatures, from about 40°F to 130°F, often referred to as the "danger zone".

This danger zone is why we refrigerate our foods until an hour or so before we are ready to cook them. It is also why we cook our foods to specific temperatures before we eat them.

The biggest misconception about bacteria and the danger zone is that any food in the temperature range is not safe and as soon as you move above 130°F the food instantly becomes safe. The truth is that the bacteria begin to die in direct relation to the temperature they are exposed to.

The best way to visualize this is to think about how we humans react to heat. We do fine in climates where the temperature is below 100°F. However, once it begins to climb around 110°F or 120°F you begin to hear about deaths in the news due to heat stroke. If the temperature were to raise to 200°F stepping outside for more than a few seconds would kill you.

Bacteria behave in the exact same way. They begin to die at around 130°F to 135°F and 165°F just about instantly kills them. You can see this in the chart below, based on the USDA data replicated in the Required Cooking Time section. At 136°F it takes

about 63 minutes for your food to be safe and at 146°F it only takes 7 minutes to become safe.

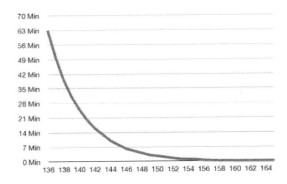

This concept is why the USDA recommends that chicken is cooked to 165°F, because at that temperature it takes only a few seconds for enough bacteria to die to achieve acceptable safety levels. In comparison, at 136°F it takes 63.3 minutes at that temperature to achieve the same safety level, something that is virtually impossible using traditional cooking methods. Using sous vide makes it possible to heat chicken and other meats to an internal temperature of as low as 130°F and hold it there long enough to kill the bacteria.

Please remember that this is assuming that your thermometer is exact and the water temperature is completely steady. I recommend always cooking foods at a little higher than the minimum temperature and a little longer than the minimum cooking time in order to account for any variance in temperature your equipment causes.

For more information about how long chicken, poultry, and beef need to be held at certain temperatures please refer to the USDA Guide mentioned in our Resources chapter. For more explanations of how this works you can reference the excellent guides by Douglas Baldwin or Serious Eats mentioned in our Resources chapter.

Plastic Safety

Another main concern of sous vide is cooking in plastic and whether or not this is a dangerous practice. Many scientists and chefs believe that cooking in food grade plastic at these low temperatures does not pose any risk, the temperature is about equivalent to leaving a bottle of water in your car, or in a semi during transport, in summer.

However, I find it hard to believe that we know everything about how plastic reacts to heat, water, our bodies, and the environment. As such, I encourage you to read up on the safety of plastic in sous vide and plastic in general and come to your own conclusions about the safety of using these techniques or consuming products packaged or shipped in plastic.

Sous Vide at BBQ Parties

If you are interested in staying up to date with sous vide you can join our free newsletter and get monthly sous vide tips and links to the best articles on the internet.

You can join our newsletter here:
http://bit.ly/ey9R5C

COOKING PARTY FOODS

Sous vide adds a lot of convenience to many different types of cooking. One of the areas this is very apparent is when having a BBQ or grilling party. You can use sous vide to free up a lot of time that you can spend hanging out instead of hovering around the grill.

There are a few different ways to utilize sous vide and we'll cover them for you here but they all share a few characteristics. And if you are one of those people (like me) who loves to hang out by the grill during the party, you can still do that while utilizing sous vide, you're just doing it because you *want* to, not because you *have* to.

BENEFITS OF SOUS VIDE

No Undercooking Worries

A huge benefit of using sous vide is the peace of mind that comes from knowing that your food is fully cooked through. There's no more worrying if the chicken is cooked through or it you're going to make the neighbors sick.

I find that during a party my focus is divided and I have trouble consistently cooking the food perfectly because I'm helping to set up tables, get people drinks, introducing people, and mingling. My internal clock gets off and it's very easy to over or under cook food.

This often leads to me overcooking food out of fear of serving my guests raw food. Sous vide completely eliminates this issue.

Awesome Tasting Food

One knock on sous vide is that many of the results can be replicated by traditional

means. In general I agree with this, but as I mentioned above during a party it can be very hard to consistently focus on the food and make sure it's coming out perfect.

If you use sous vide you don't have to worry about keeping any focus on the food. Either it's not on the grill yet or you know it's done as soon as the outside has grill marks! I've found this greatly increases the quality of my food during parties.

Cook the Food Ahead of Time

Cooking the food ahead of time is another great reason to use sous vide. It means you only have to use the grill to sear the food. This eliminates much of the cooking time during the party, guarantees perfectly cooked food, and ensures that the food will be done when everyone is ready to eat.

The Food is Ready When You Are

At a party people often want to eat at different times. This can be hard on the cook. You can make everything at once and people who aren't hungry get cold ones later. Or each time someone asks for some chicken or a burger you have to get it out of the refrigerator, season it, throw it on the grill and cook it for 10 to 15 minutes, taking you away from the party.

Sous vide eliminates most of these steps and cuts the cooking time dramatically. The cooking time is reduced to only 2 to 3 minutes and it becomes much easier to quickly cook for people.

TIPS AND TRICKS

Use the Beer Cooler Hack

First popularized by J. Kenji Lopez-Alt of Series Eats, the Beer Cooler Hack can be put to great use for parties. I'll summarize the method below but for a detailed discussion of it you can view his article directly: http://bit.ly/h1tYhl.

The Beer Cooler Hack is a great way to cheaply try out sous vide. However, even if you have good sous vide equipment you can still utilize it, especially in a party situation.

If you heat the water in a cooler to 131°F / 55°C then you can use it to hold food that was already sous vided. Even though you might want to cook your chicken or sausage at higher temperatures, once it's cooked you can safely hold it at 131°F / 55°C.

You can also use the beer cooler to bring food that has been cooked and chilled back up to temperature before grilling. Just heat the water to 131°F / 55°C and place the refrigerated food into it. Make sure that the water temperature stays above 131°F / 55°C, and you may have to add some more warm water once the food is put in.

Cook Steaks at the Lowest Temperature

Even though blind taste tests have shown almost everyone prefers a medium-rare steak (even self-proclaimed lovers of rare and people who only like medium-well), most people feel strongly about what they want. One of the biggest issues with sous vide is that unless you have multiple water baths all of the food has to be cooked at the same temperature.

The way to get around this at a party is to cook all of your steaks medium-rare. If some people want rare I'd reserve a steak for them to cook traditionally or just serve them

your perfect medium-rare steak and they should love it anyway.

Once you have all your steaks cooked you can change the temperature when you're grilling them. If they want a medium or medium-well steak you can just grill it for an extra few minutes during the searing phase.

Use Those Cheap, Tough Cuts

Buying a few ribeye steaks for the family won't break the budget but if you are having friends over expensive meat can add up fast. A great use of sous vide is to buy cheaper cuts of meat and sous vide them for a day or two. The cooking will tenderize the steaks and they will taste like much more expensive cuts of meat.

You can get top round roasts or chuck roasts for $2 to $4 dollars a pound, cook them sous vide, then slice them into 1" thick steaks. Once the party starts you can just grill them and impress all of your guests who will think you're serving high-quality meat.

Tailor to Your Guests

Since sous vide dishes can be cooked in individual pouches it allows you to tailor the portions to who is eating them. For instance, if someone is allergic to pepper or spices you can do one pouch without the pepper and the other pouches with it.

You can also use two or three different seasonings in a batch of sous vide by sealing them separately. Then you can let everyone mix and match and eat the ones they prefer.

SAMPLE PARTY FOOD MENUS

There are many great menus you can serve at parties. You can mix and match most items from this book for a party and do just fine. Here are a few ideas to get you started.

Sausage Party

Buy an assortment of sausages including kielbasa, sweet italian sausage, bratwursts, and hot italian sausage and cook them using the Basic Sous Vide Sausage recipe. Get some chicken and turkey sausages and cook them at 141°F / 60.5°C for several hours.

Buy a bunch of rolls, some good mustards, sauerkraut, and any other toppings that look good to you. Serve them buffet style so people can try different sausages, on or off the rolls, and try all the different condiments.

Kebab Party

Choose several of the kebab recipes like the Steak Kebabs, Hawaiian Chicken Kebabs, Spicy Lamb Kebabs, and the Sweet Potato and Chicken Kebabs. Cook the meat ahead of time, quick chill it, and refrigerate it. On the day of the party make all of the kebabs and once the party starts you can cook them whenever you are ready.

You can also prepare some sides like yellow or white rice, some corn on the cob, or even other finger foods. You may also want to do some veggie only kebabs if you have any vegetarians coming.

Burger Party

Cook a bunch of hamburger patties, following the Classic Hamburger recipe. Serve them with a lot of different toppings like lettuce, tomato, pickles, sautéed mushrooms, caramelized onions, bacon, different cheeses, and roasted red peppers. You can even use more unusual toppings like guacamole or pineapple.

You can set them all out and let your guests make their own hamburgers.

Another fun variation is to cook mini-burgers, or sliders, and serve them on small rolls. This allows your guests to make 2 or 3 hamburgers and sample all the different toppings.

CONVERTING EXISTING RECIPES

If you have any questions you can ask them in the Sous Vide Forums on our website. Just post your question and other sous vide cooks will weigh in with their answers.

You can find them on our website at:
www.cookingsousvide.com/sous-vide-forums

Even though we provide almost a hundred recipes in this book we know we can't cover it all. One of the great things about sous vide is that it is easy to convert existing recipes into sous vide recipes with just a few tweaks. This means you can quickly convert the recipes from your favorite grilling books into sous vide meals. There are 3 main steps to doing this.

ISOLATE SEASONINGS

To convert the recipe you first need to isolate the seasonings. Most grilled foods are seasoned ahead of time with a rub or glaze and then placed on the grill or have a sauce or crust added during or after the grilling process.

First look at the recipes and see what these seasonings are. Once you find the seasonings you need to determine whether they should be added before or after the sous vide process.

Season Before

Many recipes will call for spice rubs, marinades, or other similar seasonings. Throughout the marinating and cooking processes these flavors will melt into the meat and flavor it, and at the end of the cooking period they won't be distinct flavors.

These are the types of seasonings to add before the sous vide process. You can add the spice rubs to the meat before bagging it or place fresh rosemary and thyme directly into the bags. In general it's best to substitute powdered garlic, onion, and ginger for their fresh counterparts, otherwise they can impart an off flavor.

Season After

Often times a recipe, especially steaks, will have some sort of crust on it. While these crusts flavor the meat they don't break down during the cooking process like many rubs or marinades do. This means when you eat the meat you still get the distinct flavor and texture of the crust.

These are the types of seasonings to add after the meat is cooked sous vide. If you add a crust beforehand the moist sous vide process will quickly dissolve it. To get around this, once you take the meat out of the sous vide pouches you can dry it and then add the crust. Once you finish the grilling the crust will be very similar to a traditional one.

DETERMINE TIME AND TEMPERATURE

The next thing needed to convert a traditional recipe is the time and temperature you will need to cook it at. At the end of this book we have provided time and temperatures for several traditional grilled foods. Simply turn to the chart in the back and find your cut of meat, or a similar cut, and follow the time and temperature recommendations there.

CHOOSE YOUR FINISHING METHOD

One of the key things in most sous vide dishes is the finishing method used. The different methods add their flavors and textures to the meat. Depending on what the dish is and what you are trying to accomplish you will want to choose one of the following methods.

Grilling

Grilling is a great way to finish meat since it adds the smokey flavor and the grill marks so common in grilled foods. It's the main finishing method used in this book.

Smoking

Some recipes call for food to be smoked either before or after you grill them. You can still accomplish this by smoking it after you remove the food from the sous vide bath. For longer times or cold smoking it can be better to smoke the meat beforehand to minimize the time the food is in the danger zone.

Pan Frying

Pan frying or pan searing is the most common method of finishing sous vide meats, though we don't use it much in this book. It can usually be used instead of grilling with only a slight loss of the grilling flavor. It's usually done in oil in a hot pan on the stove. The meat is left on just long enough to brown before being removed.

Roasting

Roasting isn't as common as the other methods but it can be a great way to finish crusts or sear the top and sides of sous vide meat. It is normally done at 450°F or under the broiler. You can also do this on your grill by using very high, indirect heat.

PUTTING IT ALL TOGETHER

Now that you know all the steps it is very easy to take a recipe you love and convert it to a sous vide recipe.

Just isolate the seasonings and see if they need to be added before or after the sous vide cooking. Next, figure out the time and temperature for the food you are cooking. Finally, choose your finishing method, usually grilling or smoking for grilling recipes but it can also be searing in a hot pan or roasting.

Season your food before if it is needed. Place it in the water bath for the indicated time at the indicated temperature. Remove it from the water bath and add any post-bath seasonings. Then finish it with grilling or the method of your choice.

SOUS VIDE AND GRILLING TIPS

We have a fan page on Facebook. You can follow us there for updated recipes, tips, and equipment reviews.

You can find it at:

http://www.facebook.com/pages/Cooking-Sous-Vide/210566932301881

Easy on the Spices

Because of the length of time sous vide cooking requires, especially for the tough cuts of meat, and the effects of the vacuum seal, spices can come across much stronger than they would in a normal grilled piece of meat. It's better to err of the side of less and re-season after taking them out of the sous vide bath than to try and eat a dish that tastes only like garlic.

Ingredients, Ingredients, Ingredients

You want to know what the secret to good cooking is? Use high-quality ingredients. The better the ingredients you use the better your resulting dish will be. This is even easier with sous vide since you will be perfectly cooking the food every time and don't have to worry about ruining it.

More and more farmers markets are opening up in cities everywhere and if you are planning a nice meal the extra flavor from locally grown fruits and vegetables (and even meat) is more than worth the extra money.

Fresh is Better

Another way to improve your dishes is to be sure to use fresh ingredients. If a recipe calls for lime or orange juice, instead of using bottled juice just grab a lime and juice it for the recipe, you'll be able to taste the difference.

Turn to the Powders

Using fresh herbs and spices instead of dried ones is normally a good idea when cooking. However, with sous vide it can be better to use the dried powders in some cases. This is especially true for things like garlic and ginger because the raw form of both can sometimes create a bitterness in the final dish.

Throw Out Your Mops

When you finish sous vide meals you can apply spice rubs or glazes before you finish them on the grill. However, mop sauces and basting sauces don't work well since they prevent the meat from browning and will lead to overcooked meat. To use your favorite sauces I suggest putting a small amount of them into the sous vide pouch with the food before you sous vide it. This is a great way to get the flavor to permeate throughout the meat. One caveat though, be careful with alcohol or vinegar based mops because no evaporation will occur in the pouch. Feel free to experiment with different types and quantities to see what works best for you.

All Meat is Different

More and more people are purchasing meat from places other than the supermarket for a variety of reasons from better flavor and texture to healthier meat and more humane treatment. I'll save any lectures for another time but one thing is apparent, meat raised in different ways behaves differently when cooked. We've found that grass-fed beef roasts only need to be cooked for about one half the time of a comparable supermarket roast before they become tender. So be aware that meat from different places cooks differently because there's nothing worse than turning an expensive cut of meat to mush.

FINISHING

Always Salt and Pepper

Salt and peppering your food before vacuum sealing it will only enhance the flavors of the finished meal. It's recommended for almost every dish to add salt and pepper before cooking it and before you finish it on the grill. Don't be afraid to taste your dishes as they come together to make sure they are properly seasoned.

Don't Forget the Spice Rubs

Just because your food was already cooked with sous vide doesn't mean you have to omit spice rubs. Once the food is out of the sous vide bath and dried off you can add any of your favorite spice rubs to it. Once you add the spice rub just grill the food as specified and it should turn out great.

Paint on the Glaze

Another great way to add flavor is to apply a glaze to the food when you put it on the grill. Just apply it to the food before you grill it and make sure to flip it once or twice so the glaze can take.

Put the Grill to Use

Since you have a nice and hot grill ready for your sous vide you might as well put it to work. Use it to cook some vegetables for the meal, or add some char to dinner rolls or bread you are having. The more food you cook on the grill the more flavor the meal will have in general.

Simple Salsas are Great

If you are cooking a normal weekday meal then a quick and easy way to finish off sous vided meat is to just add a simple salsa to the top of it. This is especially easy in summer. Simply chop up some fresh vegetables like tomatoes, corn, avocado or squash, add some herbs like basil or oregano and toss together with some olive oil and a splash of apple cider or red wine vinegar. Plate the salsa on the grilled meat and you are all done. And the dish even looks fancy!

GENERAL GRILLING

Drier the Better

When trying to brown meat on the grill you want your meat to be as dry as possible to speed up the process. The easiest way to accomplish this is to use paper towels or a dish towel to pat the meat dry. This works when cooking raw meat that has been in a marinade as well. I have specially colored dish towels that I only use for this purpose and wash after each time.

Crank the Heat

When searing foods that have already been cooked sous vide you want to minimize the amount of time they are on the grill. Get your grill as hot as it can go and only cook the meat until a crust develops or it begins to get marks, no more than 1 or 2 minutes per side.

Preheat the Grill

Whether you are finishing your sous vide meat on a grill, on a stove, or in the oven under the broiler you should always preheat it. Putting the meat on a cold grill just takes it longer to sear and cooks the inside of the meat a lot more. Using only preheated cooking surfaces helps keep the cooking to the outside of the meat, leaving the inside perfectly cooked. Always use a very hot grill that has been pre-heated.

Open the Grill Lid

Often times when cooking on the grill, especially for thicker foods, you'll close the lid to keep the heat in and more evenly cook the food. When you're searing your sous vided foods you should leave the lid open, minimizing the cooking that will happen except on the side being seared.

Oil the Grill

Oiling the grill helps to efficiently transfer the heat from the grill to the meat and makes grill marks easier. It also means the meat will not stick, something that can be a problem with the shorter cooking times on the grill.

Go with the Propane

I won't get into the age old debate of charcoal vs propane. You can effectively use either to finish your sous vide food. However, if you are only searing the meat on the grill and you have access to both I would suggest going with propane. That way you aren't wasting a lot of charcoal just to cook for 5 minutes.

Use Indirect Heat for Crusts

If you are adding a crust that covers most of the meat, especially for a roast or other large cut, you can use indirect heat for it. For propane, turn off half your burners and place the meat on that side of the grill, close the lid, and let it cook for several minutes. For a charcoal grill just pile the charcoal on one side of the grill and place the meat on the other.

Either way you want the indirect heat very hot, much hotter than you would normally want indirect heat since you are just trying to set the crust, not cook the meat.

ADDING SMOKE

Give it Some Smoke

If you are preparing a BBQ-style dish it can help if you smoke the meat before sealing it. Even 30-60 minutes in the smoker can add a lot of flavor to the final dish. It's normally better to smoke the food before cooking it as opposed to afterwards because it reduces safety concerns.

Cheat on the Smoke

If you don't have a smoker or the time to smoke your food there is a quicker way to add some smokiness. Instead of smoking it you can add a small amount of Liquid Smoke to the bag prior to it being sealed. A smoking gun can also be a very useful tool.

Smoke it After the Sous Vide

You can also smoke your food after it comes out of the sous vide bath. You can't smoke it for too long due to health concerns but having it on for 30 or 45 minutes shouldn't hurt anything.

This is especially great if you are already smoking other foods. You can just take the meat out of the sous vide pouch, pat it dry, and place it into the smoker to quickly take on some great flavor.

Quick Smoke

A quick way to add post-sous vide smoke flavor is to add wood chips to your grill to create smoke. When you sear off your sous vide meat this smoke will help flavor it. It won't be a super strong smoke taste but it will definitely add some great flavor.

SALADS

If you are interested in staying up to date with the work we are doing in sous vide feel free to follow us on Twitter. We post articles we find interesting, links to new recipes, and other items of interest.

We are @jasonlogsdon_sv

COOKING SALADS

Salads cover a broad range of foods. There are the typical lettuce and dressing salads, mostly meat salads like chicken or tuna salad, and vegetable salads. Many salads can be improved upon and simplified by using sous vide.

The most common way to incorporate sous vide into salads is to use it to cook the main ingredient or the main garnish. It is often used to cook chicken or steak before adding it to the salad or to cook tougher vegetables such as potatoes or asparagus.

In this book we focus on many meat salads that can be finished on the grill to add depth of flavor to them.

TIPS AND TRICKS

Make Chilling Quick

Be sure if you are making a cold salad that you quickly chill your meats by placing them in a ½ ice ½ water bath. If you chill them slowly they could develop unwanted bacteria.

You can also cook the meat ahead of time, quick chill it, and then store it in the refrigerator until you are ready to put the salad together.

To Sear or Not to Sear

Salads are one of the few places where a post-sous-vide sear isn't always important. If you are going to cube the meat or if it's going to be covered in sauce (like a mayonnaise-based chicken salad) the lack of sear will not hurt the dish much.

That said, the extra flavor and texture a sear brings never hurts a dish.

GRILLED STEAK SALAD WITH HONEY MUSTARD DRESSING

Time: 2 to 10 Hours
Temperature: 131°F / 55°C
Serves: 2

For the Steak
1 pound sirloin steak
¼ teaspoon thyme powder
½ teaspoon garlic powder
Salt and pepper

For the Salad
½ red bell pepper, diced
4 baby bella or white button mushrooms, sliced
½ tomato, diced
Mixed greens or the lettuce of your choice

For the Dressing
3 tablespoons mayonnaise
1 tablespoon dijon mustard
1 tablespoon honey
Olive oil
Salt and pepper

This hearty steak salad calls for a honey mustard dressing but is equally good with any other flavorful dressing like blue cheese or thousand island. Grilling the steak after the sous vide also adds additional bold flavors to the salad.

Pre-Bath
Preheat the water bath to 131°F / 55°C.

Prepare the meat by trimming off any excess fat. Dust the steak with the garlic powder and thyme powder. Salt and pepper the meat then seal it and place in the water bath. Let it cook for 2 to 10 hours.

Finishing
Preheat a grill to very hot.

Make the dressing by whisking together the mayonnaise, dijon mustard, and honey. When it's combined slowly whisk in enough olive oil to mellow the flavor of the dressing to your taste. You can also add more honey or dijon to tweak the honey mustard dressing so it's the way you like it.

Assemble the salad by placing all the ingredients into a bowl or on a plate.

Remove the steak from the sous vide pouch and grill over high heat on a very hot grill. Slice into short strips. Drizzle the honey mustard dressing on the salad and add the strips of the sous vide strip steak to it. Lightly sprinkle the salad with salt and pepper and serve.

GRILLED CHICKEN CAESAR SALAD WITH CHIPOTLE DRESSING

Time: 2 to 4 Hours
Temperature: 141°F / 60.5°C
Serves: 6

For the Chicken
2 to 3 chicken breasts
1 teaspoon garlic powder
½ teaspoon ground coriander
¼ teaspoon ground ancho pepper
Salt and pepper

1 head romaine lettuce, coarsely chopped
2 cups croutons
½ cup parmesan cheese, freshly grated

For the Dressing
½ to 1 chipotle pepper in adobo sauce
1 egg yolk
2 anchovy filets
1 teaspoon Dijon mustard
1 teaspoon minced garlic
3 tablespoons fresh lemon juice
½ cup olive oil
Salt and pepper

The chipotle pepper adds a nice kick to the classic caesar dressing. You can add the chipotle pepper slowly to the dressing to make sure it's not too spicy for you. To make your own fresh croutons you can see the Pesto Turkey Breast Salad recipe. You can omit the raw egg if you prefer, use an organic, farm raised egg, or simply cook it at 135°F / 57.2°C for 75 minutes to pasteurize it.

Pre-Bath
Preheat the water bath to 141°F / 60.5°C.

In a small bowl mix together the spices. Season the chicken breasts with the salt and pepper then sprinkle with the spices. Add to the sous vide pouch and seal.

Place the sous vide pouch into the water bath and cook for 2 to 4 hours.

Finishing
First, make the dressing. Place the egg yolks, anchovies, garlic, mustard, chipotle pepper and lemon juice into a food processor and process until thoroughly mixed. With the food processor still running slowly add the oil. Add salt and pepper, tasting until the seasoning is right.

Preheat a grill to very hot.

Take the chicken out of the pouch and pat dry. Sear the chicken over high-heat on your grill, about 1 to 2 minutes per side. Remove from the heat and slice.

Place the lettuce in a large bowl. Add enough dressing to coat and toss the lettuce to evenly mix. Place the coated lettuce on individual plates. Top with the chicken, parmesan cheese, and croutons. Crack some fresh pepper on top and serve.

GRILLED CHICKEN SALAD

Time: 2 to 4 Hours
Temperature: 141°F / 60.5°C
Serves: 6

For the Chicken
2 to 3 chicken breasts
1 teaspoon garlic powder
1 teaspoon paprika
½ teaspoon ground cumin
Salt and pepper

For the Dressing
½ cup mayonnaise
2 tablespoons olive oil
1 tablespoon honey-mustard
1 tablespoon lemon juice
Salt and pepper

For the Salad
2 carrots, cut in half lengthwise then into ¼"
    slices
1 red bell pepper, diced
3 celery sticks, cut into ¼" slices
¼ cup seedless grapes, cut in half
½ cup walnuts
¼ cup fresh basil, cut into strips

This salad is a nice and light chicken salad. You can use any garnishes you prefer but here we use carrots, bell pepper, walnuts, and grapes to add sweetness and a crunch. I also like this salad with fresh snap peas or green beans.

For a more savory salad you can mix in a few roasted garlic cloves into the dressing and mash it in real good.

Pre-Bath
Preheat the water bath to 141°F / 60.5°C.

In a small bowl mix together the spices. Season the chicken breasts with the salt and pepper then sprinkle with the spices. Add to the sous vide pouch and seal.

Place the sous vide pouch into the water bath and cook for 2 to 4 hours.

Finishing
First, make the dressing. Add all of the dressing ingredients to a bowl and mix well. Add salt and pepper, tasting until the seasoning is right.

Preheat a grill to very hot.

Take the chicken out of the pouch and pat dry. Sear the chicken over high-heat on your grill, about 1 to 2 minutes per side. Remove from the heat and dice or shred it.

Place the chicken and the salad ingredients into a bowl. Top with the dressing and toss to coat evenly. Garnish with the fresh basil and serve.

GRILLED DUCK SALAD WITH APPLES

Time: 2 to 4 Hours
Temperature: 131°F / 55°C
Serves: 4

For the Duck
2 duck breasts
1 tablespoon Chinese 5-spice powder
1 teaspoon garlic powder
Salt and pepper

For the Salad
1 apple, preferable a crisp, good eating variety,
    quartered and thinly sliced
6 cups arugula or spinach, washed and dried
¼ cup pomegranate seeds
¼ cup sliced almonds, toasted
Feta cheese, crumbled

For the Vinaigrette
3 tablespoons cider vinegar
1 tablespoon honey
6 tablespoons olive oil
Salt and pepper

*Duck and apples go well together and the vinaigrette
helps to cut the fattiness from the duck. Don't prep
the apples too far ahead of time or they will begin to
turn brown. You can also serve this with a fresh
baguette or hot rolls to round out the full meal.*

Pre-Bath
Preheat the water bath to 131°F / 55°C.

Sprinkle the duck breasts with the Chinese
5-spice powder and garlic powder. Salt and
pepper them then add to the sous vide
pouches. Seal the pouches then place in the
water bath and cook for 2 to 4 hours.

Finishing
Preheat a grill to very hot.

Remove the duck breasts from the sous vide
pouches and pat dry.

Make the vinaigrette. Combine the vinegar,
honey, salt and pepper in a bowl. Then
slowly whisk in the olive oil.

On a very hot grill sear the duck breasts on
each side, about 1 to 2 minutes each. Then
cut the duck breast meat into ¼″ thick slices.

Toss the arugula with enough dressing to
coat the leaves. Divide the arugula among 4
plates. Top with the apples and duck breast.
Add 1 tablespoon of pomegranate seeds to
each plate then top with the almonds and
feta cheese.

ORANGE DUCK SALAD WITH GRILLED RADICCHIO

Time: 2 to 4 Hours
Temperature: 131°F / 55°C
Serves: 4

4 duck breasts
1 cup orange juice
½ teaspoon mustard
2 tablespoons red wine vinegar
1 tablespoon honey
½ cup olive oil
Salt and pepper
1 head of radicchio, cut in half
Mixed greens
1 sweet red bell pepper, sliced
½ pint fresh raspberries or blackberries
½ cup pecans

The acid in the orange juice helps to cut the richness of the duck breast and the berries and bell pepper add a nice sweetness to it. The radicchio also adds some needed bitterness to cut the richness.

Pre-Bath

Heat the water bath to 131°F / 55°C.

Sprinkle the duck breasts with salt and pepper. Seal the duck in the sous vide pouches and place into the water bath. Cook for 2 to 4 hours.

Finishing

In a bowl mix together the orange juice, mustard, vinegar and honey. Whisk in the olive oil to create the vinaigrette.

Heat your grill to high. Sear the radicchio halves until they soften and just begin to char. Remove from the heat and cut into ¼" slices.

Remove the duck from the sous vide pouches and pat dry. Grill for 1 to 2 minutes per side until they take on color. Remove from the heat and slice into ½" slices.

To serve, place the greens in individual bowls or on plates. Top with the bell pepper and berries. Add the radicchio and duck slices and spoon the vinaigrette on top. Add the pecans and serve.

TURKEY BREAST AND AVOCADO SALAD

Time: 1 to 4 Hours
Temperature: 147°F / 63.9°C
Serves: 4

For the Turkey
1 pound turkey breast or filets
½ teaspoon garlic powder
½ teaspoon onion powder
Salt and pepper

Arugula and Avocado Salad Ingredients
7 cups arugula or baby spinach
1 avocado, sliced
Parmigiano-Reggiano Cheese, for shaving

Lemon Vinaigrette Ingredients
2 tablespoons lemon juice
1 garlic clove, minced
⅓ cup olive oil
Salt and pepper

This is a nice and light salad with the bite of the arugula being offset by the richness of the avocado. This salad is great for a whole meal, especially if you serve it with warm rolls or a fresh baguette.

Pre-Bath
Preheat the water bath to 147°F / 63.9°C.

Salt and pepper the turkey breast filets then sprinkle with the garlic and onion powder. Seal in sous vide pouches, place in the water bath and cook for 1 to 4 hours.

Finishing
Preheat a grill to very hot.

Remove the turkey breasts from the water bath and pat dry.

Now make the vinaigrette. Combine the lemon juice and garlic in a bowl, add some salt and pepper and let sit for a few minutes. Slowly whisk in olive oil until the mixture thickens.

Sear the breasts on a very hot grill, about 1 minute per side. Remove from the heat and cut into strips.

Place the arugula in a serving bowl and add enough vinaigrette to flavor it, tossing to mix. Top the arugula with the avocado slices and chicken. Spoon a bit more dressing over them and season with salt and pepper. Using a vegetable peeler, shave strips of Parmesan cheese over the top and serve.

PESTO TURKEY BREAST SALAD

Time: 1 to 4 Hours
Temperature: 147°F / 63.9°C
Serves: 4

For the Turkey
2 turkey breasts or filets
½ teaspoon garlic powder
½ teaspoon dried basil
Salt and pepper

For the Salad
5 bacon strips, cut lengthwise ½" wide
¼ cup mayonnaise
5 tablespoons pesto
½ pint cherry tomatoes, halved
½ loaf of bread, preferably a baguette or
   sourdough
2 tablespoons olive oil
1 teaspoon garlic, minced
Salt and pepper

This is a very flavorful meal, getting a lot of complex flavors from the pesto and the homemade croutons. It's hearty enough to be served as a main course, especially if you add some romaine or bibb lettuce to it.

For an more unusually meal you can cut romaine hearts in half length-wise and grill them for 1 or 2 minutes to add color and additional flavor.

Pre-Bath
Preheat the water bath to 147°F / 63.9°C.

Salt and pepper the turkey breasts then sprinkle with the garlic powder and the dried basil. Seal in sous vide pouches, place in the water bath and cook for 1 to 4 hours.

Finishing
When the turkey is almost done, assemble the rest of the dish.

Preheat the oven to 350°F. Cut the loaf of bread into ½" to 1" cubes. Toss the cubes with olive oil, garlic, salt and pepper then place on a baking sheet with raised sides and toast them in the oven for 10 to 15 minutes. The cubes should be slightly crispy and browned but still soft on the inside. Once done remove from the oven and set aside.

Fry the bacon in a pan over medium heat until the fat is rendered and they turn crisp. Remove from the heat and drain on paper towels.

Remove the turkey breasts from the water bath and pat dry. Sear the breasts on a very hot grill for 1 minute per side. Remove from the heat and cut into strips.

Whisk together the mayonnaise and pesto in a bowl.

Place the turkey on individual serving plates. Spoon a decent amount of the mayonnaise pesto mixture on top. Top with the tomatoes, croutons and bacon strips and serve.

BLACKENED GROUPER CAESAR SALAD

Time: 15 to 30 Minutes
Temperature: 122°F / 50°C for sushi quality,
otherwise 132°F / 55.5°C
Serves: 4

For the Grouper
1 pound of grouper, cut in 4 portions
1 tablespoon butter
½ teaspoon ground cumin
½ teaspoon garlic powder
½ teaspoon onion powder
½ teaspoon ground coriander
¼ teaspoon cayenne pepper, or to taste
Salt and pepper

1 head romaine lettuce, coarsely chopped
2 cups croutons
½ cup parmesan cheese, freshly grated

For the Dressing
1 egg yolk
2 anchovy filets
1 teaspoon Dijon mustard
1 teaspoon minced garlic
3 tablespoons fresh lemon juice
½ cup olive oil
Salt and pepper

*This recipe is a take off of a traditional caesar salad
and is very good with any white, mild fish. It is a
simple summer recipe inspired by the Lazy Flamingo,
a great bar in Bokeelia, Florida we always go to when
we visit family down there. They have local, grouper
on the menu and you can get it grilled, blackened, or
fried and served on salad, a sandwich, or just plain.
My wife always gets it blackened on their Caesar
salad.*

*Here's a version of it using sous vide you can make at
home. You can also use chicken instead of fish. To make
your own fresh croutons you can see the Pesto Turkey
Breast Salad recipe. You can also use your favorite
bottle of caesar dressing to save time.*

Pre-Bath

Preheat the water bath to the indicated
temperature.

In a small bowl mix together the spices.
Season the grouper with the salt and pepper
then sprinkle with the spices. Add to the
sous vide pouch along with the butter and
seal.

Place the sous vide pouch into the water
bath and cook for 15 to 30 minutes.

Finishing

First, make the dressing. Place the egg yolk,
anchovies, garlic, mustard and lemon juice
into a food processor and process until
thoroughly mixed. With the food processor
still running slowly add the oil. Add salt
and pepper, tasting until the seasoning is
right.

Preheat a grill to very hot.

Take the grouper out of the pouch and pat
dry. Sear the grouper over high-heat on a
hot grill until just browned, about 1 minute
per side.

Place the lettuce in a large bowl. Add
enough dressing to coat and toss the lettuce
to evenly mix. Place the coated lettuce on
individual plates. Top with the grouper,
parmesan cheese, and croutons. Crack some
fresh pepper on top and serve.

GRILLED FINGERLING POTATO SALAD

Time: 30 to 60 Minutes
Temperature: 183°F / 83.9°C
Serves: 4 as a side

For the Potatoes
3 pounds small fingerling potatoes, cleaned but
   skin on
½ teaspoon pepper
1 tablespoon fresh thyme
1 teaspoon salt

For the Salad
¼ pound bacon, cut crosswise into strips
2 carrots, diced
3 shallots, diced
2 garlic cloves, diced
1 celery stalk, diced

For the Dressing
¼ cup mayonnaise
2 tablespoons apple cider vinegar
2 tablespoons Dijon mustard
Salt and pepper

2 tablespoons parsley, chopped
1 tablespoon tarragon, chopped

*This is a unique mustard-vinegar potato salad which
has a tartness not found in the typical mayonnaise
based potato salads. The vinegar also helps this dish to
complement fattier main courses like ribeye or duck
breast. Grilling the potatoes also adds more flavor to
the dish.*

Pre-Bath
Preheat the water bath to 183°F / 83.9°C.

Place the potatoes in a sous vide pouch and
add the pepper, thyme, and salt. Seal the
pouches and place in the water bath for 30
to 60 minutes, until the potatoes are tender.

Finishing
While the potatoes are cooking finish
preparing the dish.

In a pan over medium heat sauté the bacon
until it begins to crisp and the fat is
rendered. Remove half of the bacon fat from
the pan. Add the carrots, garlic, and shallots
to the pan and cook until the garlic and
shallots become soft, about 5 minutes.

Preheat a grill to very hot.

Remove the potatoes from the sous vide
pouches and grill over high heat for several
minutes until they take on some color.
Remove from the heat and place into a large
bowl. Pour the onion-garlic-bacon mixture
over the top of the potatoes and stir to mix.

In a separate container mix together the
mayonnaise, vinegar, and mustard. Pour it
on top of the potatoes and mix well.
Sprinkle the parsley and tarragon on top
and serve.

CHIPOTLE SWEET POTATO SALAD

Time: 45 to 60 Minutes
Temperature: 183°F / 83.9°C
Serves: 6 as a side

For the Potatoes
4 sweet potatoes
4 tablespoons butter
½ teaspoon ground cumin
½ teaspoon ground coriander
½ teaspoon ground cloves
½ teaspoon ancho chile powder
½ teaspoon kosher salt

For the Salad
2 cups corn kernels, cooked
2 cups canned black beans, rinsed and drained
3 shallots, diced
½ cup cilantro, chopped

For the Vinaigrette
1 chipotle chile from a can of chipotles in adobo
1 garlic clove, finely minced
2 tablespoons ketchup
6 tablespoons lime juice
1 tablespoon honey
½ cup olive oil
Salt and pepper

*The chipotle adds a nice burn to the usually super
sweet potatoes and helps turn this into a savory salad.
Finishing the potatoes on the grill also adds some
caramelization of the sugars in the potatoes for
additional flavor.*

Pre-Bath

Preheat the water bath to 183°F / 83.9°C.

Peel the sweet potatoes, add to the sous vide pouches along with the butter and the spices and seal. Cook for 45 to 60 minutes until the potatoes are soft.

Finishing

When the potatoes get close to finishing put together the rest of the salad.

First, make the dressing. Put the chipotle, garlic and ketchup into a blender and process until smooth. Add the lime juice, honey, salt and pepper, and process again. Slowly add the olive oil while processing until it is incorporated.

Warm the beans and corn either in a 350°F oven for 5 to 10 minutes or in the microwave, if you prefer.

Preheat a grill to very hot.

Remove the potatoes from the sous vide pouches and cut into quarters. Grill over high heat for several minutes until they take on some color. Remove from the heat and dice into 1" chunks.

Place into a large serving dish. Add the corn, black beans, shallots, and cilantro and mix well. Spoon the dressing over the salad, tossing and tasting as you go so you don't over dress it.

GRILLED ASPARAGUS AND WHITE BEAN SALAD

Time: 30 to 40 Minutes
Temperature: 183°F / 83.9°C
Serves: 4 as a side

For the Asparagus
½ pound asparagus
1 tablespoon butter or olive oil
Salt and pepper

For the Salad
1 14-ounce can white beans
1 or 2 roasted red bell peppers, diced

For the Vinaigrette:
2 tablespoons red wine or apple cider vinegar
1 tablespoon shallot, minced
6 tablespoons olive oil
6 tablespoons fresh basil, minced
Salt and pepper

This side salad goes really well with mahi mahi or seared tuna. It is also good with turkey or chicken. The vinaigrette adds a nice bite to the asparagus for additional flavor while the beans fill out the dish and the bell peppers add sweetness.

Pre-Bath

Preheat the water bath to 183°F / 83.9°C.

Cut the bottoms off of the asparagus. Place into the sous vide pouch, add the butter and salt and pepper then seal the pouch. Place the pouch into the water bath and cook for 30 to 40 minutes.

Finishing

Preheat a grill to very hot.

Combine the vinegar, shallot, salt, and pepper in a bowl, let sit for 3 to 5 minutes then slowly whisk in the olive oil and stir in the basil.

Take the asparagus out of the water bath and grill for several minutes until they begin to develop color. Remove from the heat and cut into 1" to 2" pieces.

Place the asparagus into a serving bowl. Add the beans and peppers and toss. Add enough vinaigrette to coat the salad and add salt and pepper as needed.

CHICKEN SAUSAGE CAPRESE SALAD

Time: 2 to 3 Hours
Temperature: 141°F / 60.5°C
Serves: 4

For the Sausage
4 chicken sausages
1 teaspoon sage

Fort he Salad
2 tomatoes, cut into ¼"-½" slices
1 or 2 balls mozzarella, cut into ¼"-½" slices
Balsamic vinegar, preferably a nice one
Olive oil, preferably a nice one
Salt and pepper
1 bunch basil, 10-14 leaves, cut into thin strips

Caprese salad is a classic summer salad and this take on it adds the chicken sausage to make it a much heartier dish while still remaining relatively light. You can also use turkey sausage for much of the same effect.

Pre-Bath
Preheat the water bath to 141°F / 60.5°C.

Place the sausages into the sous vide pouches and sprinkle with the sage. Seal the pouches then place in the water bath and cook for 2 to 3 hours.

Finishing
Heat a grill to high heat.

Remove the sausages from their pouches and pat them dry. Quickly sear them on two sides on the grill over high heat, about 1 minute per side. Remove them from the heat and slice into ¼" slices.

Lay the tomatoes out on the plate, place a slice of mozzarella on each one, then a slice or two of chicken sausage. Drizzle some olive oil and some balsamic vinegar on top. Season with salt and pepper then sprinkle the basil over top.

CAULIFLOWER WITH SPICY CHICKPEAS

Time: 20 to 30 Minutes
Temperature: 183°F / 83.9°C
Serves: 4 as a side

1 head of cauliflower
2 tablespoons butter or olive oil
Salt and pepper

For the Chickpeas
2 cups cherry tomatoes, halved
¼ red onion, thinly sliced
1 cup canned chickpeas, rinsed and drained
½ cup fresh cilantro, chopped

For the Vinaigrette
3 tablespoons lemon juice
1 serrano pepper, seeded and diced
¼ cup olive oil
Salt and pepper

Cauliflower is considered bland by many people so in this dish we use some spicy chickpeas to add some bold flavors. You can use any canned beans you have and each kind will add its own flavor to the dish. Finishing the cauliflower on the grill also introduces new flavors not usually found with cauliflower.

Pre-Bath
Preheat the water bath to 183°F / 83.9°C.

Cut the cauliflower into large pieces and place into the sous vide pouch with the butter. Salt and pepper the cauliflower and then seal the pouch. Place the pouch into the water bath and cook for 20 to 30 minutes, until soft.

Finishing
Preheat a grill to very hot.

First make the vinaigrette. Combine the lemon juice, serrano pepper, salt, and pepper in a bowl, let sit for 3 to 5 minutes then slowly whisk in the olive oil.

Remove the cauliflower from the sous vide pouch and grill for several minutes until it begins to develop color. Remove from the heat and put in a large serving bowl. Add the chickpeas, tomatoes, red onion, and cilantro. Mix well then toss with enough of the dressing to coat but not overpower it.

GRILLED BROCCOLI WITH PARMESAN AND LEMON

Time: 20 to 25 Minutes
Temperature: 183°F / 83.9°C
Serves: 4 as a side

1 head of broccoli
½ cup freshly grated Parmigiano-Reggiano
   cheese
1 lemon
Salt and pepper

*This dish uses sous vide to perfectly cook the broccoli
and then uses the grill to add some additional flavor
to it. The parmesan cheese also adds a deeper flavor
while the lemon brightens the dish up.*

Pre-Bath

Preheat the water bath to 183°F / 83.9°C.

Cut the broccoli into large pieces and place
into the sous vide pouch. Salt and pepper
the broccoli and then seal the pouch. Place
the pouch in the water bath and cook for 20
to 25 minutes.

Finishing

Preheat a grill to very hot.

Remove the broccoli from the sous vide
pouch and grill for several minutes until it
begins to develop color. Remove from the
heat, place in the serving bowl, and sprinkle
the parmesan cheese over the top. Squeeze
the lemon over the top and serve.

KEBABS

For more tips and tricks you can visit our sous vide forums.
There are a lot of questions answered and information exchanged there.

You can find them on our website here:
www.cookingsousvide.com/sous-vide-forums

COOKING KEBABS

One of the biggest issues when cooking kebabs is making sure the meat on them is fully cooked and simultaneously not burning the vegetables. Normally it's a very delicate balancing act using indirect heat, or cooking the meat on separate skewers than the vegetables.

Using sous vide allows you to pre-cook the meat then put them on the skewers for a final grilling until the vegetables are done. Even if you don't have vegetables on the skewers, using sous vide is still a great way to ensure perfectly cooked meat every time.

TIPS AND TRICKS

Try for Fast-Cooking Vegetables

When using sous vide to pre-cook your kebab meat it helps to try and focus on vegetables that cook quickly on the grill. With sous vide you normally grill the meat for only a minute or two per side, which isn't long enough to cook most vegetables. Even though it can take longer to cook even fast-cooking vegetables, the time needed is much less than vegetables like potatoes or winter squash. Some good vegetables are yellow or green summer squash, tomatoes, mushrooms, sweet onions, bell peppers, and eggplant.

Let Them Cool

If you are cooking vegetables that need to be cooked slightly longer you can let the meat cool to room temperature before grilling the kebabs, about 30 minutes, or even chill the meat in a ½ ice and ½ water bath. This will keep the meat from overcooking as the vegetables cook since most of the heat will be used to bring the meat back up to temperature.

Undercook the Meat

Another way to counteract vegetables that take awhile on the grill is to undercook the meat slightly from where you want it at the end, as long as you stay above 131°F / 55°C. The extra time on the grill will finish cooking the meat without overcooking it.

Have Fun with the Veggies

Part of the fun with kebabs is trying different vegetables. Don't be scared to try different combinations and different spices and sauces.

Season the Kebabs

Even though the main ingredient might be cooked with spices it is important to season the rest of the ingredients on the kebab. For a simple seasoning just drizzle the kebabs with olive oil and then salt and pepper them. You can also add chipotle or cayenne pepper to add a nice kick.

Quick Drying

Drying lots of 1" cubes of meat can be time consuming but it really pays off in developing a nice crust on your meat.

I recommend putting a paper towel or kitchen towel on a plate then putting the meat on it. Place another towel on top of it and gently rub the top towel in a circular motion as the meat rolls slightly under it.

The two towels will soak up most of the moisture and will speed up the drying process for you.

STEAK KEBABS WITH MIXED VEGETABLES

Time: 2 to 8 Hours
Temperature: 131°F / 55°C
Serves: 4 to 8

For the Steak
2 pounds ribeye steak, cut into 1" cubes
½ teaspoon dried thyme
½ teaspoon rosemary
½ teaspoon ancho chile powder
Salt and pepper

For the Vegetables
1 zucchini, cut into ½" thick slices
1 sweet red pepper, cut into 1" x 1" slices
1 sweet onion, cut into 1" wedges
1 pint cherry tomatoes

This is a great meal to serve in summer when the vegetables are fresh from the garden. Feel free to substitute for any vegetables you love. You can also use any type of steak you like, just adjust the cooking time accordingly. If you are having a party it is easy to substitute chuck, top round, or another tough steak and tenderize it with the sous vide.

Pre-Bath
Preheat the water bath to 131°F / 55°C.

Sprinkle the steak with the thyme, rosemary, ancho powder, salt, and pepper. Place in the sous vide pouches and cook for 2 to 8 hours.

Finishing
Heat a grill to high-heat. You won't be cooking the meat long on it, just searing it, so use the hottest setting.

Take the steak cubes out of the water bath and remove them from the pouches. Pat them dry with a paper towel or dish cloth.

Skewer the steak cubes, zucchini, pepper, onion, and tomatoes, alternating between them.

Cook the kebabs on the grill until the zucchini begins to soften, turning at least once. Remove from the heat and serve.

MOROCCAN BEEF KEBABS

Time: 2 to 4 Hours
Temperature: 131°F / 55°C
Serves: 4 to 8

2 pounds ground beef
4 cloves garlic, minced
1 medium onion, finely minced
2 teaspoons ground cumin
2 teaspoons turmeric
¼ cup fresh parsley, chopped
¼ cup fresh cilantro, chopped
1 teaspoon cinnamon
1 teaspoon chipotle chile powder
1 teaspoon black pepper
1 teaspoon salt, or to taste

These Moroccan beef kebabs are called "Kefta" and are a spicy and smoky treat. They are made out of ground beef here but ground lamb can also be used, or a combination of the two.

You can use more or less chile powder, depending on your preference for spiciness.

Pre-Bath
Preheat the water bath to 131°F / 55°C.

In a large bowl mix together all of the ingredients. Form elongated meatballs about 1" in diameter and 3" to 5" long out of the meat. The will have a similar shape to a hotdog or sausage link. Place them in the sous vide pouch and lightly seal so as not to flatten the balls.

Place in the sous vide pouches and cook for 2 to 4 hours.

Finishing
Preheat a grill to very hot.

Take the meat balls out of the water bath and remove them from the pouches. Pat them dry with a paper towel or dish cloth.

Place them onto a skewer and cook the kebabs on the grill until they brown lightly, turning at least once. Remove from the heat and serve.

SPICY LAMB KEBABS

Time: 18 to 36 Hours
Temperature: 131°F / 55°C
Serves: 4 to 6

For the Lamb
1 ½ pounds leg of lamb, cut into 1" cubes
2 teaspoons fresh parsley, chopped
2 teaspoons fresh mint, chopped
2 teaspoons ground coriander
1 teaspoon garlic, minced
1 teaspoon paprika powder
1 teaspoon salt
½ teaspoon cinnamon
½ teaspoon chipotle chile pepper
½ teaspoon ground black pepper

For the Vegetables
1 pint cherry tomatoes
1 pint pearl onions
1 pint baby bella mushrooms, de-stemmed

If you like lamb then these kebabs are for you. Cooking the lamb leg via sous vide for 18 to 36 hours results in super-tender meat. With a quick cook on the grill to finish off the vegetables the lamb should stay very moist. The spices in the lamb are pretty traditional but you can substitute anything you prefer.

This recipe is great when served with some saffron rice, Tzatziki sauce, and a simple side salad.

Pre-Bath
Preheat the water bath to 131°F / 55°C.

Mix together the lamb and all of the seasonings. Place in the sous vide pouches and cook for 18 to 36 hours.

Finishing
Heat a grill to high-heat. You won't be cooking the meat long on it, just searing it, so use the hottest setting.

Take the lamb cubes out of the water bath and remove them from the pouches. Pat them dry with a paper towel or dish cloth.

Skewer the lamb cubes and vegetables, alternating between them.

Cook the kebabs on the grill until the tomatoes begin to burst, turning at least once or twice. Remove from the heat and serve.

Hawaiian Chicken Kebabs

Time: 2 to 4 Hours
Temperature: 141°F / 60.5°C
Serves: 4 to 8

For the Chicken
2 pounds chicken, cut into 1" cubes
1 teaspoon dried orange peel
1 teaspoon mace
Salt and pepper

For the Garnish
2 cups pineapple, cut into 1" cubes
2 cups cooked ham, cut into ½" cubes

This is a twist on the classic Hawaiian pizza combination of ham and pineapple. You can use a cooked ham steak, canadian bacon slices, or sliced deli ham.

I used orange peel and mace to season the chicken to give it a little citrus flavor but you can use any seasonings you want. You can also introduce some great flavor by adding teriyaki sauce before grilling.

These kebabs are great when served with rice or a vegetable stir fry.

Pre-Bath
Preheat the water bath to 141°F / 60.5°C.

Sprinkle the chicken with the orange peel, mace, salt, and pepper. Place in the sous vide pouches and cook for 2 to 4 hours.

Finishing
Preheat a grill to very hot.

Take the chicken cubes out of the water bath and remove them from the pouches. Pat them dry with a paper towel or dish cloth.

Skewer the chicken cubes, pineapple, and ham, alternating between them.

Cook the kebabs on the grill until the meat just begins to brown and the pineapple is warmed through, turning at least once. Remove from the heat and serve.

Chicken Satay

Time: 2 to 4 Hours
Temperature: 141°F / 60.5°C
Serves: 4-6 as an appetizer

3 chicken breasts, cubed

For the Marinade
¼ cup soy sauce
¼ cup lemon juice
2 teaspoons toasted sesame oil
1 tablespoon brown sugar
2 garlic cloves, diced
½ teaspoon chipotle chile powder
2 tablespoons peanut butter
Salt and pepper

Chicken satay is a classic Thai appetizer. It has a nice peanut background and some good spice from the chipotle. They are commonly served as an appetizer with a peanut sauce for dipping.

Pre-Bath
Preheat the water bath to 141°F / 60.5°C.

Place all of the marinade ingredients in a bowl and mix well. Add the chicken and toss to coat thoroughly.

Place the chicken in the sous vide pouches and cook for 2 to 4 hours.

Finishing
Preheat a grill to very hot.

Take the chicken cubes out of the water bath and remove them from the pouches. Pat them dry with a paper towel or dish cloth.

Skewer the chicken cubes then cook on the grill until the meat just begins to brown, turning at least once. Remove from the heat and serve.

Spicy Steak Kebabs

Time: 12 to 24 Hours
Temperature: 131°F / 55°C
Serves: 4 to 8

For the Steak
2 pounds stew meat, cut into 1" cubes
½ teaspoon ground coriander
½ teaspoon ground cumin
½ teaspoon chipotle chile powder
⅛ teaspoon cayenne pepper
Salt and pepper

For the Vegetables
1 pint button mushrooms, de-stemmed
1 sweet onion, cut into 1" wedges

Cooking stew meat sous vide is a great way to save money on kebabs. The long cooking time will really tenderize the steak. The spices give it some good depth of flavor and some spicy heat. You can season them with any of your favorite spices.

Pre-Bath
Preheat the water bath to 131°F / 55°C.

Sprinkle the steak with the coriander, cumin, chipotle powder and cayenne pepper, then salt and pepper. Place in the sous vide pouches and cook for 12 to 24 hours.

Finishing
Preheat a grill to very hot.

Take the steak cubes out of the water bath and remove them from the pouches. Pat them dry with a paper towel or dish cloth.

Skewer the steak cubes, mushrooms, and onion, alternating between them.

Cook the kebabs on the grill until the mushrooms begin to soften, turning at least once. Remove from the heat and serve.

Sweet Potato and Chicken Kebabs

Time: 30 to 45 Minutes
Temperature: 183°F / 83.9°C
Serves: 4 to 8

2 sweet potatoes
1 tablespoon butter
½ teaspoon cinnamon
¼ teaspoon nutmeg
Salt and pepper

For the Chicken
2 pounds chicken, cut into 1" cubes
Salt and pepper

For the Baste
½ cup bourbon
½ cup honey

Instead of cooking the chicken sous vide we use it to cook the sweet potatoes. Since you will be grilling them until the chicken is done you want to make sure the potatoes aren't too soft when you remove them from the water bath.

You can use this method for any longer-cooking vegetables you want to use on skewers, like fingerlings potatoes.

If you use the Cook and Chill method you could cook the sweet potatoes sous vide, chill them, cook the chicken sous vide and then assemble the skewers for a final grilling.

Pre-Bath
Preheat the water bath to 183°F / 83.9°C.

Peel the sweet potatoes and cut into ¾" to 1" chunks. Add them to the sous vide pouches along with the butter and the spices and seal. Cook for 30 to 45 minutes until the potatoes just begin to soften.

Finishing
Preheat a grill to very hot.

Take the sweet potatoes out of the water bath and remove them from the pouches. Pat them dry with a paper towel or dish cloth.

Skewer the sweet potato and chicken cubes, alternating between them. Salt and pepper the skewers.

Whisk together the bourbon and honey. Use this to baste the kebabs as they cook on the grill.

Cook the kebabs on the grill until the chicken is cooked through, turning at least once and basting with the bourbon baste. Remove from the heat and serve.

CHICKEN CORDON BLEU KEBABS

Time: 2 to 4 Hours
Temperature: 141°F / 60.5°C
Serves: 4 to 8

For the Chicken
2 pounds chicken, cut into 1" cubes
½ teaspoon sage
Salt and pepper

For the Garnish
20 cubes Gruyere cheese, about ½" square
10 thinly sliced pieces of deli ham, cut in half

Here we take the classic ingredients in chicken cordon bleu and turn them into kebabs. It's a great way to get a classic dish out to the grill and for you to impress your family.

Pre-Bath
Preheat the water bath to 141°F / 60.5°C.

Sprinkle the chicken with the sage, then salt and pepper it. Place it in the sous vide pouches and cook for 2 to 4 hours.

Finishing
Preheat a grill to very hot.

Take the chicken cubes out of the water bath and remove them from the pouches. Pat them dry with a paper towel or dish cloth.

Wrap each cube of cheese with a piece of ham and skewer them along with the chicken cubes, alternating between them.

Cook the kebabs on the grill until the ham begins to darken and the cheese begins to melt. Remove from the heat and serve.

BURGERS AND SANDWICHES

We are constantly adding recipes to our website as we continue to experiment with sous vide. Maybe something there will inspire you.

You can find them at:

www.cookingsousvide.com/info/sous-vide-recipes

Cooking Burgers and Sandwiches

Burgers are a classic summer grilling food and are consumed in backyards everywhere. Sous vide allows you to perfectly cook this great food, as well as to safely eat hamburgers that are cooked medium-rare.

Sous vide is also great for chicken, turkey, or steak sandwiches since it can cook the food perfectly.

You typically cook the meat first using sous vide and then remove it from the bath, pat it dry and quickly grill it to develop some added flavors. Then you assemble the burger or sandwich as you normally would.

Tips and Tricks

Try Out Medium-Rare Burgers

One of the best parts about cooking hamburgers sous vide is the ability to safely eat them at medium-rare temperatures. Traditionally, unless they are personally ground, hamburgers should be served at medium because the bacteria from the outside of the meat gets mixed into the middle of the patty and will not be killed by searing. This is why it is fine to eat a medium-rare (or rare) steak that has been seared but medium-rare burgers are usually not served.

With the longer cooking times in sous vide you can ensure that the burger will be up to temperature long enough to kill off the harmful bacteria in the middle of the burger. This can result in a very juicy burger that

can't normally be achieved without grinding your own meat.

That said, if you prefer a more traditional doneness you can cook it at 141°F / 60.5°C and the results will still be very good

Light Sealing

When cooking hamburgers or other patties be sure to only lightly vacuum the bag. If you vacuum it too hard it can crush the patties and make them misshapen. Often times I will use the water displacement method with a ziploc bag since it results in no crushing.

Undercook Slightly

Regardless of how you want to eat your sandwiches I recommend cooking them at several degrees under your desired temperature, being sure not to go below 131°F / 55°C. This is because the meat on sandwiches and burgers is often thinner than other cuts. So to brown it well it will sometimes raise the temperature of the meat more than you would prefer. If you undercook the meat slightly then it will compensate for the raise in temperature.

One note, this is only for meat going straight from the sous vide to the grill. If you are planning on chilling the meat first then you will want to cook them at the final desired temperature.

Warm the Cheese

If you are adding cheese to your burger or sandwich it is best to let it sit out for 30 minutes to come up to room temperature. Since the food isn't on the grill very long it is hard to thoroughly melt cold cheese.

CLASSIC HAMBURGER

Time: 2 to 4 Hours
Temperature: 131°F / 55°C
Serves: 4

For the Meat
4 hamburger patties, preferably at least 1" thick
Salt and pepper

4 slices American cheese
4 tomato slices
4-8 large lettuce leaves
8 pickle slices, usually "bread and butter"
4 good hamburger buns
Mustard
Ketchup

This is the classic American burger. It's simple but when cooked perfectly it can be great. Using sous vide to pre-cook the patty creates a super moist, medium-rare hamburger that is still safe to eat. If you prefer a more traditional doneness you can cook it at 141°F / 60.5°C and the results will still be very good.

You can take this basic burger recipe and add any of your favorite toppings to it. Burgers are great with so many different things that you shouldn't be afraid to experiment.

Serving this with homemade french fries, sweet potato fries, or kettle chips is a great way to round out the meal.

Pre-Bath
Preheat the water bath to 131°F / 55°C.

Salt and pepper the patties and then lightly seal them in the sous vide pouches. Add to the water bath and cook for 2 to 4 hours.

Finishing
Heat a grill to high-heat. You won't be cooking the meat long on it, just searing it, so use the hottest setting.

Take the beef patties out of the water bath and remove them from the pouches. Pat them dry with a paper towel or dish cloth. Quickly sear the burgers on the grill for 1 minute then flip over, top with cheese, and close the lid of the grill for 2 minutes.

Remove the burgers from the heat and place on the buns. You can top with the tomato, lettuce, and pickles or serve them on the side.

Bacon-Mushroom Swiss Burger

Time: 2 to 4 Hours
Temperature: 131°F / 55°C
Serves: 4

For the Meat
4 hamburger patties, preferably at least 1" thick
Salt and pepper

4 slices swiss cheese
1 pint baby bella mushrooms
8 strips of bacon
4 good hamburger buns
Mustard
Ketchup

Mushrooms, bacon, and swiss cheese are another great pairing for hamburgers. As the hamburgers are getting close to being ready you sauté the bacon strips and then cook the mushrooms in the rendered fat, resulting in a salty, bacon-flavored hamburger.

It can also be good to serve these with lettuce and tomato to help cut the richness of the burger.

Pre-Bath
Preheat the water bath to 131°F / 55°C.

Salt and pepper the patties and then seal them in the sous vide pouches. Add to the water bath and cook for 2 to 4 hours.

Finishing
Preheat a grill to very hot.

Place the bacon strips in a pan over medium heat and cook until the fat is rendered and they are crispy. Set the bacon aside.

Pour our ½ of the rendered fat. Add the mushrooms, stirring occasionally, until they are soft, about 10 minutes.

Take the beef patties out of the water bath and remove them from the pouches. Pat them dry with a paper towel or dish cloth.

Drizzle the cut side of the buns with canola oil and place on the grill. Cook just until they start to brown and then remove from the grill.

Quickly sear the burgers on the grill for 1 minute then flip over, top with cheese, and close the lid of the grill for 2 minutes.

Remove the burgers from the heat and place on the buns. Top with 2 bacon slices and a spoonful of the mushrooms and serve.

SMOKY BBQ BACON BURGER

Time: 2 to 4 Hours
Temperature: 131°F / 55°C
Serves: 4

For the Meat
4 hamburger patties, preferably at least 1" thick
1 teaspoon paprika
½ teaspoon chipotle chile powder
1 teaspoon liquid smoke

4 slices sharp cheddar cheese
8 strips of bacon
4 good hamburger buns
Several good sweet pickles
BBQ Sauce, preferably sweet

The combination of the paprika, chipotle, and liquid smoke, as well as the bacon, will result in a very smoky, flavorful burger. This is counteracted by the sharp cheddar cheese, the tangy pickles, and the sweet BBQ sauce.

Pre-Bath
Preheat the water bath to 131°F / 55°C.

Salt and pepper the patties and sprinkle with the paprika and chipotle chile powder. Place them in the sous vide pouch and add the liquid smoke. Seal the sous vide pouch, add to the water bath, and cook for 2 to 4 hours.

Finishing
Preheat a grill to very hot.

Place the bacon strips in a pan over medium heat and cook until the fat is rendered and they are crispy. Set the bacon aside.

Take the beef patties out of the water bath and remove them from the pouches. Pat them dry with a paper towel or dish cloth. Quickly sear the burgers on the grill for 1 minute then flip over, top with cheese, and close the lid of the grill for 2 minutes.

Remove the burgers from the heat and place on the buns. Top with 2 bacon slices and the BBQ sauce and serve.

GRILLED STEAK SANDWICH WITH BALSAMIC ONIONS

Time: 2 to 8 Hours
Temperature: 131°F / 55°C
Serves: 4

For the Steak
1 ½ pounds ribeye, cut into bun-sized portions
½ teaspoon garlic powder
½ teaspoon onion powder
½ teaspoon ancho chile powder
Salt and pepper

2 onions, thickly sliced
2 tablespoons balsamic vinegar
4 sandwich rolls or buns
4 slices havarti cheese

The best part about this recipe is that you can make both the steaks and onions ahead of time. You just have to grill the steak and warm the onions before serving.

The balsamic vinegar helps add a nice tang and sweetness to the onions without overpowering their flavor. These steak sandwiches are great with steak fries or macaroni and cheese. Cooking them sous vide ensures that the steak is nice and tender and easy to bite through.

Pre-Bath

Preheat the water bath to 131°F / 55°C.

Mix the spices together in a bowl. Salt and pepper the steaks then sprinkle with the spice mixture. Seal in sous vide pouches, place in the water bath and cook for 2 to 8 hours.

Finishing

Add some canola or olive oil to a pan set over medium to heat and warm. Add the onions and salt and pepper them. Cook until they are soft, about 15 minutes. About 10 minutes into the process add the balsamic vinegar and stir well.

Remove the steaks from the water bath and pat dry. Sear the steaks on a hot grill for 1 or 2 minutes on the first side. Flip the steaks and top with the onions and cheese. Cover the grill and let cook for 1 to 2 minutes to start melting the cheese.

Place the steak on the buns and serve.

CHICKEN AND GRILLED PEPPERS SANDWICH

Time: 2 to 4 Hours
Temperature: 145°F / 62.7°C
Serves: 4

For the Chicken
4 chicken breasts
½ teaspoon paprika
½ teaspoon garlic powder
½ teaspoon onion powder
Salt and pepper

2 red bell peppers, cut into sides
4 hamburger buns or rolls
4 slices provolone cheese
4 dill pickles

These chicken sandwiches are great with the normal accompaniments for a burger such as chips or fries and potato salad. For a healthier meal you can eat it with a side of steamed veggies or a side salad.

Pre-Bath
Preheat the water bath to 145°F / 62.7°C.

Mix the spices together in a bowl. Salt and pepper the chicken breasts then sprinkle with the spice mixture. Seal in sous vide pouches, place in the water bath and cook for 2 to 4 hours.

Finishing
Heat the grill to high.

Salt and pepper the peppers and drizzle with canola oil. Place on the grill and cook until they soften and begin to char. Remove from the grill and cut into slices when they cool.

Remove the chicken breasts from the water bath and pat dry. Grill the chicken for 1 minute over high heat then flip and cover with the cheese. Close the lid of the grill and cook for another 2 minutes until the cheese just begins to melt.

Place the chicken on the buns, top with the grilled peppers, and serve with the dill pickles.

BBQ Chicken Sandwich

Time: 2 to 4 Hours
Temperature: 141°F / 60°C
Serves: 4

For the Chicken
4 chicken breasts
1 or 2 sprigs of fresh thyme
1 or 2 sprigs of fresh rosemary
½ teaspoon ancho pepper, or more for a spicier
    chicken

¼ red onion, thinly sliced
8 slices of bacon, cooked
4 slices of extra sharp cheddar cheese
4 rolls, preferably good, crusty ones
Your Favorite BBQ Sauce

This chicken sandwich has spicy chicken, crunchy onions and smokey bacon, all combined with a sweet BBQ sauce on a crusty, grilled roll. It's great when served with corn on the cob, onion rings, or macaroni and cheese.

Pre-Bath

Preheat the water bath to 141°F / 60°C.

Lightly salt and pepper the chicken breast and place in a pouch. Add the thyme and rosemary and then seal. Place the chicken breasts in the water bath and cook for around 2 to 4 hours.

Finishing

Heat your grill to high temperature when you are getting close to serving the chicken.

Drizzle the cut side of the rolls with canola oil and then place on the grill cut side down. Grill them until they begin to brown. Remove from the heat.

Remove the sous vide chicken breasts from the pouch, pat them dry with a paper towel or dish cloth and coat the with BBQ sauce. Quickly grill the chicken breasts for 1 minute then flip, top with the cheese, and close the grill for about 2 minutes. Remove from the heat.

Place the chicken on the rolls and top with the bacon and red onion.

CHICKEN BURGER WITH PEPPERS AND ONIONS

Time: 2 to 4 Hours
Temperature: 145°F / 62.7°C
Serves: 4

For the Chicken
4 ground chicken patties
½ teaspoon garlic powder
½ teaspoon onion powder
½ teaspoon ancho powder
½ teaspoon dried thyme
Salt and pepper

For the Peppers and Onions
2 tablespoons canola oil
2 onions, preferably vidalia or sweet
3-4 bell peppers - red, yellow, and orange
Salt and pepper

4 sandwich rolls or panini bread
4 slices fresh mozzarella cheese

These chicken burgers are very flavorful while still being very healthy. The bell peppers and mozzarella cheese add a lot of flavor without overpowering the chicken. They go well with coleslaw and potato salad.

Pre-Bath
Preheat the water bath to 145°F / 62.7°C.

Mix the spices together in a bowl. Salt and pepper the chicken patties then sprinkle with the spice mixture. Seal in sous vide pouches, place in the water bath and cook for 2 to 4 hours.

Finishing
Peel the onions and then cut into slices about ½" to ¾" thick, trying to keep the slices together. You can also thread the onion slices onto a shish-kabob skewer.

Cut the sides off of the peppers, leaving them in large pieces. Salt and pepper the onions and peppers and then drizzle with the canola oil.

Heat a grill to high heat. Add the onions and peppers until they just begin to brown and are cooked through.

Remove the chicken patties from the water bath and pat dry. Grill the chicken for 1 minute over high heat then flip and cover with the cheese. Close the lid of the grill and cook for another 2 minutes until the cheese just begins to melt.

Place the chicken on the buns, top with the grilled peppers and onions, and serve.

CHICKEN SANDWICH WITH SAUTÉED MUSHROOMS

Time: 2 to 4 Hours
Temperature: 145°F / 62.7°C
Serves: 4

For the Chicken
4 chicken breasts
½ teaspoon paprika
½ teaspoon garlic powder
½ teaspoon onion powder
Salt and pepper

Canola or olive oil
½ onion, thickly sliced
10 mushrooms, thickly sliced
4 hamburger buns or rolls
4 slices provolone cheese
4 dill pickles

Here we use some paprika to add a smokiness to the chicken as it is cooking sous vide.

These chicken sandwiches are great with steamed veggies or a side salad. They also go well with kettle chips or fresh french fries.

Pre-Bath
Preheat the water bath to 145°F / 62.7°C.

Mix the spices together in a bowl. Salt and pepper the chicken breasts then sprinkle with the spice mixture. Seal in sous vide pouches, place in the water bath and cook for 2 to 4 hours.

Finishing
Heat a grill to high heat.

Add some canola or olive oil to a pan set over medium heat and warm. Add the onions and mushrooms, stirring occasionally, until they are soft, about 10 minutes.

Place the buns, cut side down, on the grill and let cook until they just begin to brown. Remove from the heat.

Remove the chicken breasts from the water bath and pat dry. Grill the chicken for 1 minute over high heat then flip and cover with the cheese. Close the lid of the grill and cook for another 2 minutes until the cheese just begins to melt.

Place the chicken on the buns, top with the onions and mushrooms mixture, and serve with the dill pickles.

SPICY AND SMOKY TURKEY BURGER

Time: 1 to 4 Hours
Temperature: 147°F / 63.9°C
Serves: 4

For the Chicken
4 ground turkey patties
½ teaspoon paprika
¼ teaspoon chipotle pepper powder
Salt and pepper

½ onion, thickly sliced
10 mushrooms
½ cup BBQ sauce
4 hamburger buns
4 slices smoked gouda or smoked provolone
    cheese
4 dill pickles

The turkey is a great base for the mushrooms and onion and the BBQ sauce adds some sweetness and a little kick. These turkey burgers are great with normal burger accompaniments such as chips or fries and potato salad.

Pre-Bath
Preheat the water bath to 147°F / 63.9°C.

Salt and pepper the turkey patties then sprinkle with the paprika and chipotle pepper powder. Seal in sous vide pouches, place in the water bath and cook for 1 to 4 hours.

Finishing
Heat a grill to high heat.

Put the onions and mushrooms on the grill and cook until they just begin to brown and are cooked through. Remove them from the heat and slice the mushrooms.

Remove the turkey patties from the water bath and pat dry. Grill the turkey for 1 minute over high heat then flip and cover with the cheese. Close the lid of the grill and cook for another 2 minutes until the cheese just begins to melt.

Place the turkey burgers on the buns, top with the BBQ sauce, grilled mushrooms and onions, and serve with the dill pickles.

TURKEY AND AVOCADO SANDWICH

Time: 1 to 4 Hours
Temperature: 147°F / 63.9°C
Serves: 4

For the Turkey
4 turkey breast filets
½ teaspoon garlic powder
½ teaspoon onion powder
1 teaspoon dried orange peel
Salt and pepper

1 cup arugula
1 avocado, sliced
8 strips bacon, cooked
4 slices of provolone cheese
4 sandwich rolls

*These turkey sandwiches are nice and light. The
avocado adds some richness and the arugula adds
some crispness and bite. The dried orange peel also
lightens the flavor with a nice citrus taste.*

*You can serve this with a side salad. macaroni salad,
or fresh potato chips.*

Pre-Bath

Preheat the water bath to 147°F / 63.9°C.

Salt and pepper the turkey breast filets then
sprinkle with the garlic and onion powder
and dried orange peel. Seal in sous vide
pouches, place in the water bath and cook
for 1 to 4 hours.

Finishing

Heat a grill to high-heat. You won't be
cooking the meat long on it, just searing it,
so use the hottest setting.

Remove the turkey breasts from the water
bath and pat dry.

Sear the breasts on a very hot grill, about 1
minute per side. Remove from the heat and
top with the cheese.

Place the turkey on the buns, top with the
avocado, bacon, and arugula and serve.

SAUSAGES AND HOTDOGS

COOKING SAUSAGES AND HOTDOGS

Sausages and hotdogs are some of the most popular foods to grill. Whether they are your basic hotdogs, italian sausage, or bratwurst, they are a popular staple in backyards everywhere.

This love of sausage does come with a dark side. Next to chicken, more time is wasted worrying about whether sausages are thoroughly cooked than any other food. This also leads to regularly overcooked sausages and sausages that turn dry from being poked, prodded, and cut.

Using sous vide for your sausages will eliminate these concerns and let you serve perfectly cooked sausage every time, without fear of killing your neighbors.

The process of cooking almost any link-type of sausage is basically the same. You first cook the sausages sous vide then either quick chill them or place them directly on the grill for a few minutes, just to give the casings some color and snap.

TIPS AND TRICKS

"Rubber band" Casings

Many sausages that use natural casings, and many that use collagen casings, offer a unique challenge. The casing will not break down at the temperatures you cook your sausages at. This means that you **have** to grill or sear the sausages after you sous vide them or it will be like eating a rubber band.

On the plus side, this also means once you grill the sausage you will get the typical sausage "snap" when you bite into it since the casing will not have degraded during the cooking process.

Cooking Temperature and Time

You can cook your non-poultry sausages at any temperature you like as long as it is at or above 131°F / 55°C (poultry is generally safe at 136°F / 57.7°C) and they will be completely safe to eat if they are cooked for at least the time recommended in the "Cooking by Thickness" section.

In general, lower temperatures result in juicier and more tender sausage. But some people prefer them cooked to medium doneness, mainly due to lasting squeamishness from hearing horror stories about undercooked sausages.

In the recipes I try to use the temperatures I personally prefer but your tastes may differ so feel free to try different ones. It is fine to cook your sausages to medium if you prefer them that way, they will still be excellent.

Medium can also be the way to go if you are having guests over and don't feel like explaining to them the basics of sous vide safety in regards to time and temperature (a favorite party subject!).

Undercook Slightly

Regardless of how you want to eat your sausages I recommend cooking them at several degrees under your desired temperature, being sure not to go below 131°F / 55°C. This is because one of the best parts of sausage is the casing and in order to get it fully cooked it will sometimes raise the temperature of the sausage more than you would prefer. If you undercook the sausage slightly then it will compensate for the raise in temperature.

One note, this is only for sausages going straight from the sous vide to the grill. If you are planning on chilling the sausages first then you will want to cook them at the final desired temperature since their temperature won't be raised much during the grilling.

Hotdogs and Pre-Cooked Sausages

If you have pre-cooked your sausages using the Cook and Chill method, or if you are using store bought pre-cooked sausages (like many hot dogs) you can skip the sous vide process and just warm them up on the grill.

However, if you are cooking other things sous vide at temperatures at or lower than the final temperature of your sausage you can put them into the water bath to bring them back up to temperature before grilling them to ensure they are warmed through and not overcooked.

Check the Portions

Since sausages come in so many sizes, even within a single type, it is hard to specify how many sausages to cook for a set number of people.

For most of our sausage recipes the number indicated in the ingredients list assumes a sausage with a 1" diameter that is 5"or 6" long. If you only have smaller or larger ones you can adjust the number of sausages being used while keeping the other ingredients about the same.

BASIC SOUS VIDE SAUSAGE

Time: 2 to 3 Hours
Temperature: 137°F / 58.3°C
Serves: 4

8 italian sausage links

This is the basic sous vide sausage process. You can substitute most types of sausage for the italian sausage used here. You can also cook them at higher temperatures if you prefer, or even as far down as 131°F / 55°C for non-poultry sausages.

Pre-Bath

Preheat the water bath to 137°F / 58.3°C.

Place the sausage links in the sous vide pouches. Seal the pouches then place in the water bath and cook for 2 to 3 hours.

Finishing

Heat a grill to high-heat. You won't be cooking the sausage long on it, just searing it, so use the hottest setting.

Remove the sausage from their pouches and pat them dry. Quickly sear them on two sides on the grill over high heat, about 1 or 2 minutes per side.

Remove from the heat and serve as you normally would.

SMOKEY DOGS

Time: 2 to 3 Hours
Temperature: 141°F / 60.5°C
Serves: 4

For the Hot Dogs
6 high quality hot dogs
4 ounces butter
1 teaspoon liquid smoke

6 buns
Mustard, preferably coarse grained
Relish

This recipe adds some smokiness to the classic hot dog recipe by sealing and cooking them with liquid smoke. This addition was inspired by Chuck Friedhoff, the Executive Chef / Food & Beverage Manager of Persimmon Woods Golf Club. You can follow him on twitter at @CKFriedhoff.

The secret to a great hot dog is using high quality ingredients. Try to find the best hot dogs you can and use fresh buns.

This recipe is designed for raw hot dogs but will even add a lot of flavor to pre-cooked hot dogs.

Pre-Bath
Preheat the water bath to 141°F / 60.5°C.

Place the hotdogs into the sous vide pouches and evenly split the butter and liquid smoke between them. Seal the pouches then place in the water bath and cook for 2 to 3 hours.

Finishing
Heat a grill to high heat.

Remove the hotdogs from their pouches and pat them dry. Quickly sear them on two sides on the grill over high heat, about 1 minute per side.

Remove the hot dogs from the heat and place on a bun. Drizzle some mustard on the hot dog and serve with a spoonful of the relish on top.

Italian Sausage with Onions and Peppers

Time: 2 to 3 Hours
Temperature: 137°F / 58.3°C
Serves: 4

8 italian sausage links

2 onions
1 red pepper
1 orange pepper
1 poblano pepper
Salt and pepper

Using sous vide to cook the sausage in this classic dish of sausage and peppers ensures a moist, perfectly cooked sausage. You can also eat this dish on a hoagie roll with melted provolone cheese on top.

These sausages are also great if you are having pasta. Simply add the sausages (and even the onions and peppers) to your favorite marinara sauce for a hearty meal.

Pre-Bath

Preheat the water bath to 137°F / 58.3°C.

Place the sausage links in the sous vide pouches. Seal the pouches then place in the water bath and cook for 2 to 3 hours.

Finishing

About 15 minutes before the sausage is done start to make the onions and peppers.

Peel the onions and then cut into slices about ½" to ¾" thick, trying to keep the slices together. You can also thread the onion slices onto a shish-kabob skewer.

Cut the sides off of the peppers, leaving them whole. Salt and pepper the onions and peppers and then drizzle with the canola oil.

Heat a grill to high heat. Add the onions and peppers and cook until they just begin to brown and are cooked through. Remove them from the heat. Once they have cooled enough to handle slice the peppers into ½" strips.

Remove the sausage from their pouches and pat them dry. Quickly sear them on two sides on the grill over high heat, about 1 or 2 minutes per side.

Plate the dish by spooning the peppers and onions onto a plate and topping with 2 sausage links per person. Serve with some warm bread or a baguette.

Beer and Brats

Time: 2 to 3 Hours
Temperature: 141°F / 60.5°C
Serves: 4

8 bratwurst links
5 ounces of beer, preferably a lager

This simple recipe was inspired by the classic beer and bratwurst recipes where bratwurst is simmered in the beer. I call for the beer to be a lager but if you opt for a dark beer it can add even more complex flavors.

Sealing the brats with the beer was inspired by Chuck Friedhoff, the Executive Chef / Food & Beverage Manager of Persimmon Woods Golf Club. You can follow him on twitter at @CKFriedhoff.

Because this dish relies so heavily on the brats you should only use ones of high quality.

Once they are cooked you can eat them anyway you choose. They are great on hoagie rolls with onions and mustard, or served with sauerkraut and potato salad.

Pre-Bath
Preheat the water bath to 141°F / 60.5°C.

Place the bratwurst into the sous vide pouches and evenly split the beer between them. Seal the pouches then place in the water bath and cook for 2 to 3 hours.

Finishing
Heat a grill to high heat. Remove the bratwurst from their pouches and pat them dry. Quickly sear them on two sides on the grill over high heat, about 1 or 2 minutes per side.

Remove from the heat and serve as you normally would. These brats are great on a bun with sauerkraut and good mustard, cut up into a pasta dish, or served plain with french fries or potato salad.

TURKEY SAUSAGE GRINDER

Time: 2 to 3 Hours
Temperature: 141°F / 60.5°C
Serves: 4

For the Sausage
4 turkey sausages, about 1" diameter
1 teaspoon thyme
1 teaspoon ancho pepper

6 hoagie or sub rolls, cut to hold the sausage
4 slices provolone cheese
Honey mustard

This recipe takes turkey sausages and turns them into a more filling and flavorful meal. It's very easy to put together and will definitely impress the neighbors because the sous vide will ensure they are moist and juicy.

For some extra flavor you can also top them with guacamole.

Pre-Bath
Preheat the water bath to 141°F / 60.5°C.

Place the sausages into the sous vide pouches and sprinkle with the thyme and ancho pepper. Seal the pouches then place in the water bath and cook for 2 to 3 hours.

Finishing
Heat a grill to high heat.

Place the rolls on the grill, cut side down, and cook until they begin to char. Remove from the heat and place the cheese on them.

Remove the sausages from their pouches and pat them dry. Quickly sear them on two sides on the grill over high heat, about 1 minute per side.

Place a sausage on each roll and top with the honey mustard.

CHICKEN SAUSAGE WITH TOMATO-BASIL SALSA

Time: 2 to 3 Hours
Temperature: 141°F / 60.5°C
Serves: 4

For the Sausage
4 to 6 chicken sausages, about 1" diameter
1 teaspoon sage

For the Salsa
2 tomatoes, diced
1 bunch basil, chopped
1 tablespoon balsamic vinegar
1 tablespoon olive oil
Salt and pepper

Here we take the classic pairing of basil, tomato, and chicken and turn it into a hearty grilled meal. The tomato-basil salsa is very simple and quick to put together and works best when good, fresh tomatoes are used.

For more variation you can use other fresh vegetables in the salsa including corn, red onion, and shallots. You can also add another twist by serving this meal on a hoagie roll.

Pre-Bath
Preheat the water bath to 141°F / 60.5°C.

Place the sausages into the sous vide pouches and sprinkle with the sage. Seal the pouches then place in the water bath and cook for 2 to 3 hours.

Finishing
Heat a grill to high heat.

While the grill is heating make the salsa. Mix together the tomato, basil, balsamic vinegar, and olive oil in a bowl. Salt and pepper it and mix well.

Remove the sausages from their pouches and pat them dry. Quickly sear them on two sides on the grill over high heat, 1 to 2 minutes per side.

Serve the chicken sausages whole with the salsa spooned on top of it.

Duck Sausage with Fruit and Nuts

Time: 2 to 3 Hours
Temperature: 141°F / 60.5°C
Serves: 4

For the Sausage
4 to 6 duck sausages, about 1" diameter
1 teaspoon sage

For the Salad
1 cup spinach
½ cup sliced almonds
½ cup dried apricots, diced
½ cup apple, diced
1 tablespoon honey
1 teaspoon apple cider vinegar
1 tablespoon olive oil
Salt and pepper

Duck goes with so many different flavors and here we use almonds, apricots, and apple to add depth of flavor and different textures. We also mix in some spinach for body and honey and vinegar to round out the flavors. It's very fast to put together.

Pre-Bath

Preheat the water bath to 141°F / 60.5°C.

Place the sausages into the sous vide pouches and sprinkle with the sage. Seal the pouches then place in the water bath and cook for 2 to 3 hours.

Finishing

Heat a grill to high heat.

While the grill is heating make the fruit and nut side salad. Mix together the spinach, almonds, apricots, apple, honey, vinegar, and olive oil in a bowl. Salt and pepper it and mix well.

Remove the sausages from their pouches and pat them dry. Quickly sear them on two sides on the grill over high heat, 1 to 2 minutes per side.

Serve the sausages with the fruit and nut salad on top.

LAMB SAUSAGE PITA

Time: 2 to 3 Hours
Temperature: 141°F / 60.5°C
Serves: 4

For the Sausage
4 to 6 lamb sausages, about 1" diameter
1 teaspoon paprika
1 teaspoon ancho pepper

4 pitas
1 cup watercress
1 fennel bulb, sliced
1 red onion, thinly sliced
½ cup tzatziki sauce

Lamb sausage is less common than the other types of sausage and it can be a great addition to your grilling repertoire. We serve the sausage on a pita with fennel, red onion, and tzatziki sauce but you can also serve it plain or as a topping for a salad.

Pre-Bath
Preheat the water bath to 141°F / 60.5°C.

Place the sausages into the sous vide pouches and sprinkle with the paprika and ancho pepper. Seal the pouches then place in the water bath and cook for 2 to 3 hours.

Finishing
Heat a grill to high-heat. You won't be cooking the meat long on it, just searing it, so use the hottest setting.

Remove the sausages from their pouches and pat them dry. Quickly sear them on two sides on the grill over high heat, 1 to 2 minutes per side.

Smear the tzatziki sauce on the pita. Place a sausage on the pita and top with the fennel, red onion, and watercress.

CLASSIC BBQ

Interested in sous vide shirts, aprons, and mugs?
We have a bunch of different gear you can buy in our online store.

You can find the sous vide gear at:
www.zazzle.com/cooking_sous_vide

COOKING CLASSIC BBQ

For all the BBQ purists out there we'd like to acknowledge that sous vide cannot perfectly replicate traditional BBQ results, smoking meat for hours, cooking over low heat, basting the whole time. There are some things that have to be done the traditional way in order to replicate the excellent results they are known for.

That said, sous vide can get you a lot closer to traditional BBQ than most other methods of cooking. It's also very easy to do and results in consistently great flavor and moist meat without having to worry about or tend to the food.

So if you love being out by the grill or smoker all day creating great BBQ, then you should probably skip this chapter. But if you're looking for a quick way to make some great food and don't feel like firing up the smoker, these recipes will help get you started.

TIPS AND TRICKS

Adding Smoke
There are a few ways to add smoke to your barbecue.

1) Use a smoker or grill with wood chips to smoke the meat for a few hours before sous viding.

2) When sealing the meat in the sous vide pouch add Liquid Smoke to it.

3) Use a smoker or grill to smoke the food after it comes out of the sous vide. This should only be done for a short amount of time.

Chopped Instead of Shredded
Many BBQ recipes will call for shredding the meat before serving it. This will work for some sous vide recipes but in general it is easier to finely chop the meat. It will result in a similar texture but is much easier to do when you are cooking your meat medium rare instead of well done.

Dry Rubbed BBQ Beef

Time: 1 to 2 Days
Temperature: 131°F / 55°C
Serves: 4 to 6

For the Beef
2-3 pounds top round roast, cut into 1 ½" slabs
1 cup BBQ sauce

For the Rub
5 tablespoons brown sugar
¼ cup paprika
4 tablespoons salt
3 tablespoons freshly ground black pepper
1 ½ tablespoons garlic powder
1 tablespoons onion powder
½ teaspoon mustard powder
½ teaspoon cayenne pepper
½ teaspoon celery seeds

This sweet rub has a hint of heat and works well on most kinds of beef. It's also good on chicken and pork.

Using a tough roast cut of beef like this for steaks helps save money, especially when cooking for a large number of people. The sous vide process will help tenderize it enough that it will taste like a higher quality steak.

Pre-Bath
Preheat the water bath to 131°F / 55°C.

Mix together all the rub ingredients in a bowl then coat the slabs of roast with it. Any extra rub can be kept in a sealed container in a cabinet for several months.

Add the roast slabs to the sous vide pouches and then seal. Place in the water bath for 1 to 2 days. For a grass-fed roast 12 to 24 hours should be good.

Finishing
Preheat a grill to very hot.

Take the beef slabs out of the water bath and remove them from the pouches. Pat them dry with a paper towel or dish cloth. Quickly sear the slabs on the grill for about 1 to 2 minutes per side. Brush both sides with the BBQ sauce and grill for 30 seconds on each side.

Take the beef off the grill, slice into strips and serve. It is great served with macaroni and cheese, coleslaw, or potato salad. It is also excellent when sliced and served on some fresh rolls with cheddar cheese and more BBQ sauce.

"Smoked" Beef Brisket

Time: 1 to 3 Days
Temperature: 135°F / 57.2°C
Serves: 4 to 8

3-4 pound brisket
1 tablespoon liquid smoke

For the Rub
2 tablespoons ground cumin
2 tablespoons garlic powder
2 tablespoons onion powder
2 tablespoons ground coriander
1 teaspoon chipotle powder

If you enjoy smoking foods you can omit the liquid smoke and then manually smoke the brisket before you put it in the water bath or even for a little bit before you serve it.

This brisket is great with any normal BBQ sides like cole slaw or potato salad. For even more flavor you can serve it with your favorite BBQ sauce. Leftovers are fantastic on nice rolls when topped with melted cheese, diced onions, and BBQ sauce.

Pre-Bath

Preheat the water bath to 135°F / 57.2°C.

Mix together all the rub ingredients in a bowl then coat the brisket with it. Any extra rub can be kept in a sealed container in a cabinet for several months.

Add the brisket to the sous vide pouch along with the liquid smoke and then seal. Place in the water bath for 1 to 3 days. For a grass-fed brisket 24 to 36 hours should be good.

Finishing

Preheat a grill to very hot.

Take the brisket out of the water bath and remove it from the pouch. Pat it dry with a paper towel or dish cloth. Quickly sear the brisket on the grill for about 1 to 2 minutes per side.

Take the brisket off the grill, slice into ⅛" to ¼" strips, and serve.

Beef Ribs with Balsamic-Basil Sauce

Time: 2 to 3 Days
Temperature: 131°F / 55°C
Serves: 4

For the Ribs
3-4 pounds of beef ribs
2 teaspoons garlic powder
2 teaspoons onion powder
4 rosemary sprigs
4 thyme sprigs
Salt and pepper

For the Sauce
3 tablespoons balsamic vinegar
½ teaspoon finely minced garlic
⅓ cup fresh basil leaves
½ cup olive oil
Salt and pepper

2 tablespoons fresh basil leaves, coarsely
    chopped, for garnish

*These beef ribs have a nice tang to them from the
sauce. Cooking them for such a long time results in
super tender meat. You can also cook them for a
shorter time if you prefer them to have more chew to
them. They go well with a side of mashed potatoes or
roasted vegetables.*

Pre-Bath
Preheat your sous vide water bath to 131°F /
55°C.

Salt and pepper the ribs and sprinkle with
the garlic and onion powders. Place in a
sous vide pouch and add the thyme and
rosemary. Seal the pouches and place in
your water bath. Let it cook for 2 to 3 days.

Finishing
Place all the ingredients for the sauce into a
blender or food processor and process until
thoroughly combined.

Remove the beef ribs from the sous vide
pouches and pat them dry with a paper
towel or dish cloth. Quickly sear the ribs on
a hot grill for about 1 to 2 minutes per side,
until just browned. Brush the ribs with the
sauce and cook for 1 minute longer per side.

Place the ribs on individual plates, spoon
the sauce over them, sprinkle with the
remaining basil, and serve.

"Smoked" Chicken Breast

Time: 2 to 4 Hours
Temperature: 141°F / 60°C
Serves: 4

4 chicken breasts
1 teaspoon paprika
½ teaspoon ancho chile powder
1 teaspoon liquid smoke
Salt and pepper

This sous vide chicken recipe will result in a smoky and moist chicken. It's also incredibly simple to do. It goes great with some macaroni and cheese and corn on the cob.

For a more dramatic presentation you can get bone-in chicken breasts.

Pre-Bath

Preheat the water bath to 141°F / 60°C.

Lightly salt and pepper the chicken breast and season with the paprika and ancho powder. Place in a pouch and add the liquid smoke then seal. Place the chicken breasts in the water bath and cook for around 2 to 4 hours.

Finishing

Heat your grill to high temperature when you are getting close to serving the chicken.

Remove the sous vide chicken breasts from the pouch, pat them dry with a paper towel or dish cloth. Quickly grill the chicken breasts for 1 or 2 minutes per side, just enough time to develop some color. Remove from the heat and serve.

PULLED PORK WITH VINEGAR SAUCE

Time: 1 to 2 Days
Temperature: 135°F / 57.2°C
Serves: 5 to 10

For the Pork
4-5 pounds pork shoulder, trimmed of excess fat
1 tablespoon ancho chile powder
1 tablespoon cumin
1 tablespoon coriander
1 tablespoon liquid smoke
1 tablespoon Worcester sauce
Salt and pepper

For the Vinegar Sauce
1 cup cider vinegar
¾ cup water
2 tablespoons sugar
1 tablespoon red pepper flakes
2 shallots, diced
2 tablespoons salt
1 teaspoon pepper

*This pulled pork can be eaten plain and also makes
excellent sandwiches. You can also replace the vinegar
sauce with your favorite BBQ sauce for a sweeter
meal. I normally serve it with a side of cornbread,
coleslaw and some mac and cheese.*

Pre-Bath
Preheat the water bath to 135°F / 57.2°C.

Mix the spices together in a bowl. Salt and
pepper the pork shoulder, then coat with the
spices. Place it in the pouch with the
Worcester sauce and liquid smoke. Seal the
pouch and place in the water bath. Let it
cook for 1 to 2 days.

Finishing
When you're getting close to serving the
pork you will want to make the sauce.
Whisk together all of the ingredients in a
bowl.

Remove the pork roast from the sous vide
pouch pat dry. Quickly sear the pork on all
sides on a hot grill, about 1 or 2 minutes per
side. Remove from the heat and chop with a
knife until in small pieces.

Serve with a spoonful of the vinegar sauce
over top.

"FALLING OFF THE BONE" RIBS

Time: 8 to 12 Hours
Temperature: 135°F / 57.2°C
Serves: 2 to 4

2 pounds of back or baby back ribs
1 tablespoon celery salt
1 tablespoon paprika
½ tablespoon garlic powder
½ tablespoon freshly ground black pepper
½ tablespoon ancho chile powder
Salt

These ribs are simple to make and very flavorful. You can also glaze them with BBQ sauce when you are searing them for even more flavor. They are great for parties since you can cook them ahead of time and just throw them on the grill when everyone starts to get hungry.

Pre-Bath

Preheat the water bath to 135°F / 57.2°C.

In a bowl mix together all the spices. Cut the ribs into pieces that will easily fit into your sous vide bags. Sprinkle salt on the ribs and then coat them with ½ of the spice mix.

Place the ribs into the sous vide pouches and then seal. Be sure you don't seal the ribs too tightly or the bones may pierce the bag. Place in the water bath and cook for 8 to 12 hours, until they are very tender.

Finishing

Preheat a grill to very high heat.

Remove the sous vide pouches from the water bath and take the ribs out of the sous vide pouches. Pat them dry and then sprinkle the meaty side with the remaining spice rub.

Quickly grill the ribs just until the meat is seared, about 1 to 2 minutes per side. Take off the grill and serve.

BEEF STEAKS AND ROASTS

COOKING BEEF STEAKS AND ROASTS

There's nothing quite like a great steak fresh off of the grill. It's one of the classic backyard foods and is great with just salt and pepper, or spruced up with a great spice rub, glaze, or BBQ sauce.

Using sous vide to cook your steaks helps you turn out perfect food every time without much effort.

Roasts are something that are not commonly done on the grill. Mastering the direct and indirect heat needed to properly cook the inside of the roast, brown the outside, and sufficiently tenderize it is very, very difficult. However, using sous vide to pre-cook the meat opens up this whole realm of foods to your grill.

TIPS AND TRICKS

Give the Tenderization Time

Most steaks can be cooked sous vide for 2 to 4 hours and will result in a more tender version of how that steak traditionally tastes. However, for some tougher steaks longer cooking times can result in steak with tenderness rivaling tenderloin with no loss of the full, beefy flavor these cuts are known for. Most roasts also need the longer cooking times to fully tenderize.

Remember Meat Differences

It is also good to keep in mind that meat of different quality cooks at different speeds. For instance, most grass fed beef cooks faster and needs less time to tenderize. You can see our *Doneness Range* section for more information.

Try Medium Rare

Even though blind taste tests have shown almost everyone prefers a medium-rare steak (even self-proclaimed lovers of rare and people who only like medium-well), most people feel strongly about what they want.

Many people enjoy medium-rare sous vide steaks even though they prefer medium or rare steaks. I recommended cooking most steaks and roasts at 131°F / 55°C to 135°F / 57°C.

That said, if you prefer a more medium doneness you can cook it at 141°F / 60.5°C and the results will still be very good.

SMOKY RIBEYE WITH SPICY SWEET MINT GLAZE

Time: 2 to 8 Hours
Temperature: 131°F / 55°C
Serves: 2

For the Steak
1-1 ½ pounds ribeye steak
½ teaspoon chipotle powder
½ teaspoon powdered thyme
½ teaspoon sweet paprika
Salt and pepper

For the Glaze
4 tablespoons mustard, preferably Dijon
1 ½ tablespoons bottled horseradish
6 mint leaves
3 tablespoons honey
Salt and pepper

These steaks combine the smoky-heat of chipotle peppers with the sharp bite of horseradish and mustard. These flavors work great with ribeye steaks because the richness of the fat helps to cut the heat. They can also be used with other tender cuts of steak or even help spice up chicken breasts or pork chops. They are great when served with some pureed sweet potatoes or sweet corn on the cob.

Pre-Bath
Preheat the water bath to 131°F / 55°C.

Sprinkle the chipotle powder, thyme, and paprika on the steaks then salt and pepper them. Add to the sous vide pouches, seal and place in the water bath. Cook the steaks for 2 to 8 hours.

Finishing
Preheat a grill to high heat.

Whisk together all the glaze ingredients in a small bowl and set aside. Remove the steaks from the sous vide pouches and pat dry. Coat the steaks with the glaze and quickly grill for 1 to 2 minutes per side, brushing on more glaze when you turn them. Remove from the heat and serve.

HERBED BUTTER SIRLOIN STEAK

Time: 3 to 10 Hours
Temperature: 131°F / 55°C
Serves: 4

For the Steak
1-2 pounds sirloin steak
1 teaspoon dried thyme
1 teaspoon cumin powder
Salt and pepper

For the Butter
½ stick butter, softened at room temperature
1 tablespoon fresh parsley, finely chopped
1 tablespoon fresh basil, finely chopped
1 tablespoon fresh tarragon, finely chopped
⅛ teaspoon ground black pepper

The herbs in this butter add some lightness to the dish while the butter adds great richness. You can substitute any of the herbs and try out other combinations you like.

Pre-Bath
Preheat the water bath to 131°F / 55°C.

Salt and pepper the steaks then sprinkle with the cumin and dried thyme. Add to the sous vide pouches and then seal and place in the water bath. Cook the steaks for 3 to 10 hours.

Finishing
To make the butter place all of the butter ingredients in a bowl and mix and mash thoroughly using a fork.

Take the steaks out of the pouches and pat dry. Sear them on a very hot grill for 1 to 2 minutes per side. Place the steaks on a plate and top with a dollop or two of the butter.

GRILLED GARLIC-ROSEMARY ROAST

Time: 12 to 24 Hours
Temperature: 131°F / 55°C
Serves: 4-6

For the Sous Vide Roast
3-4 pound sirloin roast
1 tablespoon garlic powder
1 tablespoon paprika powder
1 teaspoon ancho chile powder
2 thyme sprigs
2 rosemary sprigs

For the Crust
8 garlic cloves, peeled
4 rosemary sprigs
4 thyme sprigs
2 tablespoons sweet marjoram
2 tablespoons olive oil

It is very hard to cook an entire sirloin roast on the grill. Luckily sous vide allows us to have medium rare meat with a smoky, grilled outside. It's also a great way to impress your guests.

Cooking with sous vide allows you to keep the entire roast the doneness you want. For extra flavor you can apply a rub or paste to the outside of the roast before grilling it. I prefer a nice garlic, rosemary, and thyme paste but many people love a horseradish or mustard crust on their roast beef.

I used a sirloin roast for this sous vide recipe but you can use any large roast cut of beef. For some of the tougher cuts of beef you might want to increase the time spent in the sous vide.

Pre-Bath

Preheat the water bath to 131°F / 55°C.

Cover the sirloin roast with salt, pepper, the garlic, paprika and ancho chile powders and place in a pouch. Add the thyme and rosemary to the sous vide pouch and then seal. Place the sirloin roast in the water bath and cook for 12 to 24 hours.

Finishing

40 to 60 minutes before the roast is done wrap the garlic cloves in aluminum foil with some olive oil and salt and place in a 400°F oven or on your grill for 30 to 45 minutes, until soft. Remove and set aside to cool.

Right before the sous vide roast is done make the paste for the crust. Combine all the crust ingredients in a food processor and pulse until it forms a thick paste.

Heat your grill to high heat.

Take the sous vide sirloin roast out of the water bath and remove it from the pouch. Pat it dry with a paper towel or dish cloth. Smear the sides and top of the meat with the paste. Place the roast on the grill and cook using indirect heat until the crust just begins to set, about 5 minutes total.

Remove the roast from the grill, cut it into thin slices and serve. It goes well with mashed potatoes, a side salad, or mixed vegetables. It is also great on hamburger buns as a sliced beef sandwich. You can even save some of the juice from the sous vide pouch and use it as a dipping au jus.

BEEF FAJITAS

Time: 2 to 12 Hours or 1 to 2 Days
Temperature: 131°F / 55°C
Serves: 4 to 6

For the Steak
1-2 pounds flank steak
1 teaspoon ground cumin
1 teaspoon ground coriander
1 teaspoon garlic powder
½ teaspoon ancho chile powder
Salt and pepper

For the Pepper Onion Sides
2 tablespoons canola oil
2 onions, preferably vidalia or sweet
3 bell peppers - green and red
1-2 poblano peppers
Salt and pepper

Optional Sides
10 tortilla wrappers
6 cups sliced lettuce
4 tomatoes, diced
Refried beans
Mexican rice
Grated cheddar cheese
Sour cream

When it comes to fajitas everyone has their own preference for what goes into them. We've listed some of the optional sides but feel free to serve your fajitas with whatever you like best.

I prefer my flank steak to have some bite to it so I normally cook it for 2 to 12 hours but some people prefer it to be meltingly tender and cook it for 1 to 2 days.

Pre-Bath
Preheat the water bath to 131°F / 55°C.

Salt and pepper the steaks then sprinkle the cumin, coriander, garlic powder, and ancho powder on top. Add to the sous vide pouches then seal and place in the water bath. Cook the steaks for 2 to 12 hours.

Finishing
Peel the onions and then cut into slices about ½" to ¾" thick, trying to keep the slices together. You can also thread the onion slices onto a shish-kabob skewer.

Cut the sides off of the bell and poblano peppers, leaving the sides whole. Salt and pepper the onions and peppers and then drizzle with the canola oil.

Heat a grill to high heat. Add the onions and peppers until they just begin to brown and are cooked through.

When the onions get close to being done take the steak out of the pouch and pat dry with a paper towel or dish towel. Sear it on the hot grill for 1 to 2 minutes per side. Slice the steak on the bias and serve with the onions and peppers, tortilla wrappers, and any of the other sides you want.

"Impress the Neighbors" Steak

Time: 36 to 48 Hours
Temperature: 131°F / 55°C
Serves: 4 to 8

3 pound Top Round Roast, cut into 1 ½" slabs
2-4 sprigs rosemary
⅔ cup BBQ sauce
Salt and pepper

The best way to win over your neighbors? Serve them great steaks. They never have to know you used inexpensive meat instead of filet mignon!

This recipe shows a great way to take an inexpensive and tough cut of meat and turn it into tender steaks. Here we add BBQ sauce for extra flavor but you can use any typical steak seasonings you prefer.

Pre-Bath
Preheat the water bath to 131°F / 55°C.

Salt and pepper the meat then add it to the sous vide pouches. Place the rosemary sprigs and ½ of the BBQ sauce in the pouches and then seal. Place in the water bath for 36 to 48 hours. For a grass-fed roast 18 to 36 hours should be good.

Finishing
Preheat a grill to very hot.

Take the beef slabs out of the water bath and remove them from the pouches. Pat them dry with a paper towel or dish cloth. Quickly sear the slabs on the grill for 1 to 2 minutes per side. Brush both sides with the BBQ sauce and grill for 30 seconds on each side.

Take the beef off the grill and serve as you would a steak. It is great with potato salad or french fries.

STEAKS WITH CHIMICHURRI SAUCE

Time: 2 to 12 Hours
Temperature: 131°F / 55°C
Serves: 4 to 6

For the Steak
2 pounds flank steak
½ teaspoon onion powder
½ teaspoon garlic powder
Salt and pepper

For the Chimichurri Sauce
1 bunch parsley
9 garlic cloves
3 tablespoons onion, diced
5 tablespoons cider vinegar
4 tablespoons water
2 teaspoons dried oregano
1 teaspoon hot pepper flakes, or to taste
Salt and pepper
1 cup olive oil

These Argentinian inspired steaks take advantage of the garlicky chimichurri sauce and are excellent when served with chunky mashed potatoes or rice. The chimichurri sauce also works great with chicken or pork.

Pre-Bath
Preheat the water bath to 131°F / 55°C.

Sprinkle the onion powder and garlic powder on the steaks then salt and pepper them. Add to the sous vide pouches, seal and place in the water bath. Cook the steaks for 2 to 12 hours.

For the Chimichurri Sauce
Put the parsley and garlic in a food processor and process until finely chopped. Add the rest of the ingredients, except for the olive oil, and process until lightly mixed. Add the oil in a thin stream while processing until the sauce comes together.

Finishing
Take the steaks out of the pouches and pat dry. Sear them on a very hot grill for 1 to 2 minutes per side. Slice the flank steak on the bias and place on a plate. Spoon the chimichurri sauce over the top and serve.

HERB CRUSTED RIB STEAK

Time: 2 to 8 Hours
Temperature: 131°F / 55°C
Serves: 2

For the Steak
1-1 ½ pounds rib steak, cut into two portions
Salt and pepper

For the Rub
¼ cup dried rosemary
1 tablespoon dried oregano
1 tablespoon dried basil
1 tablespoon dried parsley
1 tablespoon sage
1 tablespoon dried garlic flakes
¼ cup coarse salt (kosher or sea)
2 tablespoons cracked black pepper

The dried herbs in this rub help to add some nice depth of flavor to the meat especially when the grill chars them lightly. This steak pairs nicely with a crisp green salad or even with a side of angle hair pasta with garlic and olive oil.

Pre-Bath
Preheat the water bath to 131°F / 55°C.

In a bowl mix together all of the ingredients for the rub. Sprinkle the rub on the steak then salt and pepper them. Add to the sous vide pouches, seal, and place in the water bath. Cook the steaks for 2 to 8 hours.

Finishing
Heat a grill to high-heat. You won't be cooking the meat long on it, just searing it, so use the hottest setting.

Remove the steaks from the sous vide pouch and pat dry. Quickly grill for 1 to 2 minutes per side, just until browned. Remove from the heat and serve.

GRILLED TUSCAN ROAST BEEF

Time: 3 to 6 Hours
Temperature: 131°F / 55°C
Serves: 4 to 8

3 pounds whole tenderloin or tenderloin roast

For the Rub
¼ cup fresh rosemary
¼ cup fresh oregano
3 tablespoons fresh parsley
2 tablespoons fresh thyme
2 garlic cloves, coarsely chopped
2 tablespoons salt
2 tablespoons black pepper
½ cup olive oil

Cooking a whole tenderloin on the grill is a great way to impress your guests. You can also use tougher cuts of meat to save money, just be sure to cook them longer.

This recipe uses bold herbs to add a lot of flavor to the normally blander tenderloin. You can use any spice rub you prefer. A spicy ancho pepper and cumin rub would also help to kick up the flavor.

Pre-Bath
Preheat the water bath to 131°F / 55°C.

First make the Tuscan rub by putting all of the rub ingredients into a food processor and process until mixed.

Rub the tenderloin with the Tuscan rub and place in the sous vide pouch. Seal the pouch and place in the water bath for 3 to 6 hours.

Finishing
Preheat a grill to very hot.

Take the tenderloin out of the water bath and remove it from the pouch. Pat it dry with a paper towel or dish cloth. Quickly sear it on the grill for 1 to 2 minutes per side.

Take the tenderloin off the grill and slice serving portions off of it. It is great with mashed potatoes, brussels sprouts, or green beans.

GRILLED FILET MIGNON WITH CREAMY GORGONZOLA

Time: 2 to 4 Hours
Temperature: 131°F / 55°C
Serves: 4

For the Steak
4 portions of filet mignon, about 1 to 1 ½ pounds
4 thyme sprigs
2 rosemary sprigs
Salt and pepper

For the Blue Cheese
¼ cup gorgonzola cheese
2 tablespoons heavy cream
1 tablespoons lemon juice
4 tablespoons olive oil
Salt and pepper

Since filet mignon is normally a blander cut of meat it can normally use a pick-me-up. Blue cheese is a classic paring but here we go with gorgonzola. This sauce really helps to add some richness to the otherwise lean filet. The grilling process will also add some flavor to the steak.

For a cheaper alternative you can use this sauce with a tougher cut of meat like in our "Impress the Neighbors" Steak.

Pre-Bath

Preheat the water bath to 131°F / 55°C.

Salt and pepper the steaks then add to the sous vide pouches. Add the thyme and rosemary then seal and place in the water bath. Cook the steaks for 2 to 4 hours.

Finishing

To make the gorgonzola cheese sauce place all of the ingredients in a food processor and process until smooth.

Take the steaks out of the pouches and pat dry. Sear them on a very hot grill for 1 to 2 minutes per side. Place the steaks on a plate and spoon the blue cheese sauce over the top and serve.

Ribeye with Spring Salsa

Time: 2 to 8 Hours
Temperature: 131°F / 55°C
Serves: 4

For the Steak
4 portions of ribeye steak, 1 ½ to 2 pounds total
1 teaspoon dried thyme
2 teaspoons garlic powder
Salt and pepper

For the Salsa
1 cup cherry tomatoes, halved
1 cup corn kernels, cooked
¼ red onion, diced
¼ cup basil, diced
1 tablespoon white wine vinegar
1 tablespoon olive oil
Salt and pepper

This spring salsa is very simple to make and really adds some lightness and flavor to the dish. It's great in late spring when the cherry tomatoes are just starting to ripen.

Pre-Bath
Preheat the water bath to 131°F / 55°C.

Salt and pepper the steaks then sprinkle with the garlic powder and dried thyme. Add to the sous vide pouches then seal and place in the water bath. Cook the steaks for 2 to 8 hours.

Finishing
To make the salsa mix all of the ingredients in a bowl. It's best to make the salsa right before you take the steaks out of the water bath.

Take the steaks out of the pouches and pat dry. Sear them on a very hot grill for about 1 to 2 minutes per side. Place the steaks on a plate and top with a spoonful or two of the salsa.

FLANK STEAK WITH POBLANO-ONION SALSA

Time: 2 to 12 Hours or 1 to 2 Days
Temperature: 131°F / 55°C
Serves: 4 to 6

For the Steak
1-2 pounds flank steak
1 teaspoon dried thyme
1 teaspoon ground coriander
½ teaspoon ancho chile powder
Salt and pepper

For the Salsa
2 tablespoons canola oil
2 onions, thickly sliced
2 poblano peppers, sliced
4 garlic cloves, minced
½ cup chicken stock
¼ cup cilantro, chopped
Salt and pepper

The chicken stock helps add a deepness of flavor to the poblano-onion salsa. The poblano peppers also add a mild heat to the dish. I prefer my flank steak to have some bite to it so I normally cook it for 2 to 12 hours but some people prefer it to be meltingly tender and cook it for 1 to 2 days.

You can cook the poblano-onion salsa ahead of time and reheat it before serving.

Pre-Bath
Preheat the water bath to 131°F / 55°C.

Salt and pepper the steaks and sprinkle with the coriander, ancho powder, and dried thyme. Add them to the sous vide pouches then seal and place in the water bath. Cook the steaks for 2 to 12 hours.

Finishing
Heat the oil in a pan over medium to medium-high heat. Add the onions and cook until they just begin to brown. Add the poblano peppers and cook until they soften. Stir in the garlic and chicken stock and cook until reduced, a few minutes. Stir in the cilantro and remove from the heat.

Take the steaks out of the pouches and pat dry. Sear them on a very hot grill, about 1 to 2 minutes per side. Cut the steak into ¼" to ½" strips and place on a plate. Top with several spoonfuls of the poblano-onion salsa.

RIBEYE STEAK WITH TOMATILLO SALSA

Time: 2 to 8 Hours
Temperature: 131°F / 55°C
Serves: 4 to 6

For the Steak
1-2 pounds flank steak
1 teaspoon dried thyme
1 teaspoon cumin powder
Salt and pepper

For the Salsa
4-8 tomatillos, 1-2 cups, diced
1 cup corn kernels, cooked
½ cup cilantro, chopped
1 shallot, diced
1 tablespoon cider vinegar
1 tablespoon olive oil
Salt and pepper

The tomatillo salsa adds a nice tang to complement the beefiness of the flank steak while the corn adds a sweet undertone and a little crunch. This dish is complemented nicely by refried beans and yellow rice.

Pre-Bath

Preheat the water bath to 131°F / 55°C.

Salt and pepper the steak then sprinkle with the cumin and dried thyme. Add to the sous vide pouches then seal and place in the water bath. Cook the steak for 2 to 8 hours.

Finishing

To make the salsa mix all of the salsa ingredients in a bowl. It's best to make the salsa right before you take the steaks out of the water bath.

Take the steaks out of the pouches and pat dry. Sear them on a very hot grill for about 1 to 2 minutes per side. Cut the steak into ¼" to ½" strips and place on a plate. Top with a spoonful or two of the salsa.

Red Wine Marinated Beef Ribs

Time: 2 to 3 Days
Temperature: 137°F / 58.3°C
Serves: 4 to 8

3-4 pounds of beef ribs

For the marinade
2 cups red wine
2 cups water
½ cup salt
½ cup brown sugar
1-2 tablespoons chipotle powder

This marinade helps infuse the ribs with even more moisture and flavor than they normally have. You can also play around with the spices in the marinade and see what flavors you like best. It's simple and fast to put together. These ribs go well with roasted vegetables and polenta.

You can do the marinating and sous vide cooking days before you are planning on grilling and with only a few minutes on the grill they will be done.

Pre-Bath

Whisk together all of the marinade ingredients. Put the ribs into one or more ziploc bags and pour the marinade over top. Place in the refrigerator for 3 to 5 hours.

Preheat the water bath to 137°F / 58.3°C.

Remove the ribs from the marinade and place them into the sous vide pouches. Seal the pouches and place in the water bath. Cook for 2 to 3 days.

Finishing

Heat a grill to high-heat. You won't be cooking the meat long on it, just searing it, so use the hottest setting.

Take the ribs out of the water bath and remove them from the pouches. Pat them dry with a paper towel or dish cloth. Quickly sear the ribs a hot grill for about 1 to 2 minutes per side, until just browned. Remove from the heat and serve.

GARLIC-HERB STEAK

Time: 1 to 2 Days
Temperature: 131°F / 55°C
Serves: 4

2 pounds top round steak, cut into serving
   portions
1 teaspoon garlic powder
1 teaspoon dried basil
1 teaspoon dried oregano
1 teaspoon dried parsley
1 teaspoon ground cumin
Salt and pepper

*This recipe takes a tough cut of meat and tenderizes it
nicely. It is great when served with grilled potatoes or
asparagus, or a light salad. You can also try different
spice combinations to see what you like best.*

Pre-Bath

Preheat your sous vide water bath to 131°F /
55°C.

Sprinkle the garlic powder, cumin, basil,
oregano, and parsley on the steak and then
salt and pepper it. Place it into the sous vide
pouch and seal it. Put into the the water
bath and cook for 1 to 2 days.

Finishing

Heat a grill to high-heat. You won't be
cooking the meat long on it, just searing it,
so use the hottest setting.

Take the steaks out of the pouches and pat
dry. Sear the steaks on the grill until just
browned, 1 to 2 minutes per side. Remove
from the heat and serve.

SPICY CHILE RIBEYE

Time: 2 to 8 Hours
Temperature: 131°F / 55°C
Serves: 4

2 pounds of ribeye, cut into serving portions
1 teaspoon ancho powder, or more to taste
½ teaspoon chipotle powder, or more to taste
¼ teaspoon cayenne powder, or more to taste
1 teaspoon garlic powder
1 teaspoon paprika powder
Salt and pepper

The three different chile powders in this rub really spice up the steaks. The ancho and chipotle both bring a smokiness to the meat with additional fruity taste from the ancho. The cayenne adds some straight heat to complement the other spices.

These spicy and smoky ribeye steaks are great when served with mashed potatoes, macaroni and cheese, or macaroni salad.

Pre-Bath

Preheat your sous vide water bath to 131°F / 55°C.

Mix the spices into a bowl and then sprinkle on the ribeye. Place it into the sous vide pouch and seal it. Place into the water bath and cook for 2 to 8 hours.

Finishing

About 15 minutes before taking the steaks out of the sous vide preheat a grill to high heat. You won't be cooking the meat long on it, just searing it, so use the hottest setting.

Take the steaks out of the pouches and pat dry. Sear the sous vide steaks on the grill until just browned, 1 to 2 minutes. Remove from the heat and serve.

FLANK STEAK WITH GRILLED ONIONS AND PEPPERS

Time: 2 to 12 Hours or 1 to 2 Days
Temperature: 131°F / 55°C
Serves: 4 to 6

For the Steak
1-2 pounds flank steak
1 teaspoon dried thyme
1 teaspoon ground coriander
½ teaspoon ancho chile powder
Salt and pepper

For the Peppers and Onions
2 tablespoons canola oil
2 onions, preferably vidalia or sweet
3-4 bell peppers - red, yellow, and orange
Salt and pepper

I prefer my flank steak to have some bite to it so I normally cook it for 2 to 12 hours but some people prefer it to be meltingly tender and cook it for 1 to 2 days. Grilling the onions and peppers add even more charred flavor to the dish.

The flank steak has a very beefy flavor that is complemented by the sweetness of the onions and peppers. I recommend using assorted bell peppers but if you prefer one over the others feel free to only use it.

Pre-Bath
Preheat the water bath to 131°F / 55°C.

Salt and pepper the steaks then sprinkle with the coriander, ancho powder, and dried thyme. Add to the sous vide pouches then seal and place in the water bath. Cook the steaks for 2 to 12 hours.

Finishing
Peel the onions and then cut into slices about ½" to ¾" thick, trying to keep the slices together. You can also thread the onion slices onto a shish-kabob skewer.

Cut the sides off of the peppers, leaving them whole. Salt and pepper the onions and peppers and then drizzle with the canola oil.

Heat a grill to high heat. Add the onions and peppers until they just begin to brown and are cooked through.

When the onions get close to being done take the steaks out of the pouches and pat dry with a paper towel or dish towel. Sear them on the hot grill for 1 to 2 minutes per side. Place the steaks on a plate and top with the onions and peppers.

THYME-GARLIC SIRLOIN STEAK

Time: 3 to 10 Hours
Temperature: 131°F / 55°C
Serves: 4

For the Steak
4 portions of sirloin steak, about 1 to 1 ½ pounds
    total
1 teaspoon garlic powder
4 thyme sprigs
Salt and pepper

For the Butter
½ stick butter, softened at room temperature
3 garlic cloves, finely minced
1 tablespoon fresh thyme, minced
⅛ teaspoon ground black pepper

*This butter topping helps add great richness to the
steak and imparts some more flavor, especially the
sharp bite from the garlic. If there is leftover butter
you can refrigerate it for several days or store it in the
freezer for up to a month.*

Pre-Bath
Preheat the water bath to 131°F / 55°C.

Salt and pepper the steaks then sprinkle
with the garlic powder and thyme. Add to
the sous vide pouches then seal and place in
the water bath. Cook the steaks for 3 to 10
hours.

Finishing
To make the butter place all of the butter
ingredients in a bowl and mix and mash
thoroughly using a fork.

Heat a grill to high-heat. You won't be
cooking the meat long on it, just searing it,
so use the hottest setting.

Take the steaks out of the pouches and pat
dry. Sear them on a very hot grill for 1 to 2
minutes per side. Place the steaks on a plate
and top with a dollop or two of the butter.

CHICKEN AND POULTRY

You can stay up to date with the current happenings in sous vide by reading our blog. We try to update it regularly with current information about sous vide.

You can find it at:
www.cookingsousvide.com/info/sous-vide-blog

Cooking Chicken and Poultry

Overcooked, bland, and dried out chicken is a common grilling stereotype for a reason. With practice it is possible to perfectly grill chicken but it is always a fine line between perfect and overcooked. Using sous vide always results in uniformly tender chicken that is very moist.

Also, much like sausage, there is usually a lot of worry about whether it is thoroughly cooked and it is often overcooked. Using sous vide gives you the peace of mind that your chicken is fully cooked.

The FDA states that chicken is safe when it is held at 136°F / 57.9°C for over 63 minutes, or 140°F / 60°C for over 30 minutes. Even though it is possible to cook chicken at those temperatures we have found that the texture is very different and tastes "raw". To avoid this we recommend chicken breasts cooked at 141°F / 60.5°C for 1 to 4 hours and legs or thighs cooked at 147°F / 64°C for 2 to 5 hours which results in a more traditional texture.

Tips and Tricks

Separate the Skin

If you love crispy skin, whether it's for chicken, duck, or fish, it can be hard to crisp properly with sous vide. A great work around is to remove the skin before you cook the food. Then as it gets close to time to remove the food from the water bath you can put the skin in the oven on a raised sheet pan and cook it at 350°F to 400°F for 15 to 20 minutes for super-crispy skin. Just place it on top of the food when you serve it and no one will ever know you cheated.

Cook Them Separately

While you can definitely cook both chicken thighs / legs and breasts at the same time it is usually better to cook them separately. I feel dark meat is best around 147°F / 64°C while white meat is best at 141°F / 60.5°C.

GRILLED CHICKEN MOLE

Time: 2 to 4 Hours
Temperature: 141°F / 60.5°C
Serves: 8

For the Chicken
8 chicken breasts
Salt and pepper

For the Mole
8 assorted medium-heat dried chile peppers such
    as ancho, mulato, and pasilla
1-2 dried chipotle chilies
1 onion, coarsely chopped
4 garlic cloves, peeled
4 plum or roma tomatoes
3 tablespoons slivered almonds
2 tablespoons sesame seeds
½ teaspoon black peppercorns
1 teaspoon coriander seeds
1 cinnamon stick
2 whole cloves
½ teaspoon aniseed or fennel seed
¼ cup fresh cilantro, chopped
1 ½ ounces golden raisins
2 cups chicken stock
¼ cup olive oil
1-2 ounces dark or unsweetened chocolate
1 tablespoon honey
1 tablespoon apple cider vinegar

*Mole is one of my favorite sauces, especially when
done right. This is a more traditional preparation than
the more mild and sweet versions found at chain
restaurants. This dish takes advantage of the different
chile flavors and is very bold and full flavored.*

*This mole is best served with some kind of rice or
bread to soak up the wonderful sauce. It is also very
good with chicken thighs whose richness stands up
well to the bold flavors. Just increase the temperature
to 148°F and cook for 2 to 5 hours. Pork shoulder can
also be used in the recipe. You can also use this mole
sauce on a mexican pizza instead of tomato sauce.*

Pre-Bath
Preheat the water bath to 141°F / 60.5°C.

Salt and pepper the chicken breasts then seal
in the sous vide pouches. Place in the water
bath and cook for 2 to 4 hours.

For the Mole Sauce
You can make the mole sauce while the
chicken is cooking or make it up to a week
ahead of time and refrigerate it.

Roast the chilies for 2 minutes per side in a
dry pan over medium-high heat until
fragrant. Set aside to cool.

On a sheet pan with sides roast the
tomatoes, onion, and garlic in an oven set at
400°F until the onions soften, 10 to 20
minutes. Set aside to cool.

Add the almonds, sesame seeds,
peppercorns, coriander, cinnamon, cloves,
and aniseed to a pan and toast over medium
heat until fragrant and just starting to
brown, about 2 minutes. Set aside to cool.
Once cool add them to a spice grinder or
food processor. Process to a fine powder.

Cut the roasted chilies in half and remove
the seeds and stems. Put them in enough hot
water to cover them. After 30 minutes drain
them.

In a food processor place the tomatoes,
onion, garlic, chilies, ground spices, cilantro,
and raisins. Process until it becomes a
smooth paste, adding water if it is too thick.

Heat the olive oil in a large saucepan with
high sides over medium heat. Add the puree
from the food processor and cook for 5
minutes, stirring constantly, until it thickens.

Reduce the heat to medium low and add the chicken stock, chocolate, honey, and vinegar and stir to combine then salt to taste. Simmer the sauce for 10 minutes while stirring occasionally until it becomes thick but still pourable.

Any excess mole will keep for about a week in the refrigerator.

Finishing

If the mole was made ahead of time then reheat it in a deep pan, otherwise, continue from the steps above.

Heat a grill to high heat. Take the chicken from the sous vide pouches and quickly grill them to develop marks.

Place a chicken breast on a plate and spoon mole sauce on top. It's best when served over rice or with tortilla shells.

JAMAICAN JERK CHICKEN THIGHS

Time: 2 to 5 Hours
Temperature: 148°F / 64.4°C
Serves: 8

2-3 pounds of chicken thighs

For the Jerk Paste
3-10 habanero or Scotch bonnet chilies, stemmed
    and cut in half
1 onion, coarsely chopped
2 bunches scallions (white and green parts),
    trimmed and coarsely chopped
5 garlic cloves, coarsely chopped
½ cup fresh parsley, coarsely chopped
½ cup fresh cilantro, chopped
2 teaspoons fresh ginger, chopped
2 tablespoons coarse salt
2 tablespoons fresh thyme
1 tablespoon ground allspice
½ teaspoon ground cinnamon
½ teaspoon freshly grated nutmeg
1 teaspoon freshly ground black pepper
¼ cup brown sugar
½ cup fresh lime juice
¼ cup olive oil
2 tablespoons soy sauce
¼ cup cold water, or as needed

Chicken thighs stand up great to this traditional Jamaican jerk flavoring but it can also be used on breasts or even pork chops or pork shoulder. A side of rice and beans or mashed plantains is a great complement to this dish. Any leftover paste can be stored in the refrigerator for about a week.

For the Jerk Paste
Add all of the dry ingredients to a food processor and process to a coarse paste. Add the remaining liquid ingredients and process until the paste becomes spreadable.

Pre-Bath
Preheat the water bath to 148°F / 64.4°C.

Smear the chicken thighs all over with the jerk paste. Add the thighs to the sous vide pouches, seal, and place in the water bath. Cook for 2 to 5 hours.

Finishing
Preheat a grill to high heat.

Take the thighs out of the sous vide pouches and pat dry. Cook them at high heat for 1 to 2 minutes per side. Remove from the heat and serve.

CHICKEN TERIYAKI FAJITAS

Time: 2 to 4 Hours
Temperature: 141°F / 60.5°C
Serves: 4

For the Chicken
4 chicken breasts
3 tablespoons teriyaki sauce
½ teaspoon ancho powder
½ teaspoon ground cumin
Salt and pepper

For the Onions and Mushrooms
20 mushrooms, preferably baby bella
2 onions
2 tablespoons canola oil
Salt and pepper

Optional Sides
10 tortilla wrappers
2 avocados, sliced
Grated Monterey jack cheese
Mexican rice
Refried beans
Sour cream

We use teriyaki here to help flavor the chicken and add some sweetness to an otherwise heavy dish.

When it comes to fajitas everyone has their own preference for what goes into them. We've listed some of the optional sides but feel free to serve your fajitas with whatever you like best.

Pre-Bath
Preheat the water bath to 141°F / 60.5°C.

Mix the spices together in a bowl. Salt and pepper the chicken breasts then sprinkle with the spice mixture. Seal in sous vide pouches with the teriyaki sauce, place in the water bath and cook for 2 to 4 hours.

Finishing
Peel the onions and then cut into slices about ½″ to ¾″ thick, trying to keep the slices together. You can also thread the onion slices onto a shish-kabob skewer.

Heat a grill to high heat. Add the onions and mushrooms until they just begin to brown and are cooked through. Remove from the heat, slice the mushrooms, and place in a serving dish.

Remove the chicken breasts from the water bath and pat dry. Quickly grill the chicken breasts for 1 or 2 minutes per side, just enough time to develop some color. Remove from the heat and cut into ¼″ slices.

Serve with the mushrooms and onions, tortilla wrappers, and any optional sides.

BBQ Chicken Thighs

Time: 2 to 5 Hours
Temperature: 148°F / 64.4°C
Serves: 4

6 chicken thighs
½ teaspoon pepper
1 tablespoon garlic powder
3 sprigs of thyme
1-2 cups BBQ sauce
Salt and pepper

These chicken thighs are very quick to put together and have great flavor, especially if you have a good BBQ sauce. They pair well with watermelon, green beans, or wild rice.

Pre-Bath

Preheat the water bath to 148°F / 64.4°C.

Trim most of the excess fat off of the thighs. Evenly distribute the garlic powder over them, then salt and pepper each one. Place the chicken thighs in the pouches with one half of a thyme sprig per thigh then seal them. Cook the chicken thighs for 2 to 5 hours.

Finishing

Heat a grill to high-heat. You won't be cooking the thighs long on it, just searing them, so use the hottest setting.

Remove the thighs from the pouch, blot dry with a paper towel, and place on a plate. Smear a light layer of the BBQ sauce on the thighs then place on the grill and cook for 1 to 2 minutes, until the sauce starts to blacken and the thighs have a good sear on them.

Remove the thighs from the grill, smear another light layer of BBQ sauce on them and serve with the rest of the sauce on the side.

TERIYAKI CHICKEN WINGS

Time: 2 to 5 Hours
Temperature: 148°F / 64.4°C
Serves: 4

2 pounds chicken wings
3 tablespoons Chinese 5-spice powder
1-2 cups teriyaki sauce
1 cup fresh cilantro, chopped
Salt and pepper

These chicken wings are easy to cook and have great flavor. I use a good bottled teriyaki sauce but you can always make your own. You can also substitute BBQ or honey-mustard and they will turn out great.

Pre-Bath

Preheat the water bath to 148°F / 64.4°C.

Dust the chicken wings with the 5-spice powder then place in the pouches. Seal the pouches and cook for 2 to 5 hours.

Finishing

Heat a grill to high-heat. You won't be cooking the wing long on it, just searing them, so use the hottest setting.

Remove the chicken from the pouch, blot dry with a paper towel, and place on a plate. Smear a light layer of the teriyaki sauce on the chicken then place on the grill and cook for 1 to 2 minutes, until the sauce starts to blacken and the wings have a good sear on them.

Remove the wings from the grill, smear another light layer of teriyaki sauce on them and top with the cilantro. Serve with the rest of the sauce on the side.

Blackened Cajun Chicken

Time: 2 to 4 Hours
Temperature: 141°F / 60.5°C
Serves: 6

6 chicken breasts

For the Rub
½ cup coarse salt (kosher or sea)
2 tablespoons freshly ground black pepper
¼ cup paprika
2 tablespoons garlic powder
1 ½ tablespoons onion powder
1 tablespoon cayenne pepper, or to taste
1 tablespoon dried thyme
1 teaspoon freshly ground white pepper
1 teaspoon ground bay leaf

This is a traditional blackening rub that adds a spicy and flavorful kick to sometimes bland chicken breasts. It is very good when served with traditional sides like collard greens, coleslaw, and macaroni salad.

For the Rub

For the rub combine all the ingredients in a bowl and stir or whisk to mix. Any left over rub can be stored in a jar or tupperware container for several months in a cabinet.

Pre-Bath

Preheat the water bath to 141°F / 60.5°C.

Sprinkle the chicken breasts on both sides with the rub, place in the sous vide pouches and seal. Place the pouches into the water bath and cook for 2 to 4 hours.

Finishing

Heat a grill to high-heat. You won't be cooking the chicken long on it, just searing them, so use the hottest setting.

Remove the chicken from the pouch and blot dry with a paper towel. Place on the grill and cook for 1 to 2 minutes on each side. Remove from the heat and serve.

BBQ Chicken Breast

Time: 2 to 4 Hours
Temperature: 141°F / 60°C
Serves: 4

4 chicken breasts
1 or 2 sprigs of fresh thyme
1 or 2 sprigs of fresh rosemary
½ teaspoon ancho pepper, or more for a spicier
  chicken
Your Favorite BBQ Sauce

*This sous vide chicken recipe will result in a
fantastically moist BBQ chicken. It's also incredibly
simple to do. The chicken goes great with some rice
and a crispy salad, or macaroni and cheese and corn
on the cob.*

Pre-Bath

Preheat the water bath to 141°F / 60°C.

Lightly salt and pepper the chicken breast
and place in a pouch. Add the thyme and
rosemary and then seal. Place the chicken
breasts in the water bath and cook for
around 2 to 4 hours.

Finishing

Heat your grill to high temperature when
you are getting close to serving the chicken.

Remove the sous vide chicken breasts from
the pouch, pat them dry with a paper towel
or dish cloth and coat the with BBQ sauce.
Quickly grill the chicken breasts for 1 or 2
minutes per side, just enough time to
develop some color. Remove from the heat
and serve.

LIME-CURRY CHICKEN THIGHS

Time: 2 to 5 Hours
Temperature: 148°F / 64.4°C
Serves: 4

4 chicken thighs
Salt and pepper

For the Butter
½ cup unsalted butter, softened at room
    temperature
1 lime, zest and juice
1 tablespoon honey
1 tablespoon red curry paste
½ teaspoon soy sauce
½ teaspoon rice wine or apple cider vinegar
¼ cup fresh cilantro, chopped
Salt and pepper

*The lime curry butter adds a rich, complex flavor to
the already moist and tender chicken thighs. You can
use more or less curry paste depending on how hot
you want your thighs to be. Or for an extra kick you
can add some cayenne pepper to the butter.*

Pre-Bath
Preheat the water bath to 148°F / 64.4°C.

Sprinkle salt and pepper on the chicken
thighs and place into the sous vide pouches.
Seal the pouches and place in the water bath
for 2 to 5 hours.

Finishing
About 10 minutes before the thighs are done
make the lime-curry butter. Add the red
curry paste, lime zest and juice, butter,
honey, vinegar, soy sauce, cilantro, and some
salt and pepper into a bowl. Mix together
thoroughly.

Take the chicken thighs out of the sous vide
pouches and pat dry. Sear over high heat on
a grill. Put a chicken thighs on a plate and
place a spoonful of the lime-curry butter on
top and serve.

Sweet Licorice Duck Breasts

Time: 2 to 4 Hours
Temperature: 131°F / 55°C
Serves: 4

4 duck breasts
3 whole star anise
2 cinnamon sticks
3 tablespoons Sichuan peppercorns
2 tablespoons fennel seeds
1 teaspoon whole cloves

This recipe calls for freshly toasted and ground spices which adds a lot more depth and character than using pre-ground spices. However, if you don't have the time or inclination to do this it is still excellent with pre-ground spices, or even a pre-mixed 5-spice Chinese powder with some extra fennel seeds added.

Pre-Bath

In a pan set over medium-low heat add the spices and toast for 3 to 5 minutes until they become fragrant. Remove from the heat and once cooled grind them in a spice grinder.

Heat the water bath to 131°F / 55°C.

Rub the duck breasts with ¾ of the rub, reserving some to be used later. Seal the duck in the sous vide pouches and place into the water bath. Cook for 2 to 4 hours.

Finishing

Remove the duck from the sous vide pouches and pat dry. Cover 1 side with the spice rub and grill over high heat, about 1 to 2 minutes per side. Remove from the heat and serve.

HOT AND SMOKY DUCK LEGS

Time: 3 to 6 Hours
Temperature: 131°F / 55°C
Serves: 4

1 pound of duck legs
Salt and pepper

For the Marinade
3 roma tomatoes
4 garlic cloves, peeled
½ onion, coarsely chopped
½ cup lime juice
3 tablespoons orange juice
2 tablespoons apple cider or red wine vinegar
3 canned chipotle chilies in adobo sauce
1 teaspoon dried oregano
1 teaspoon salt
½ teaspoon ground cumin
½ teaspoon ground coriander
½ teaspoon black pepper

The rich duck legs hold up well to bolder flavors and here we pair chipotle chilies with citrus juices to complement them. You can add more or less chipotle chillies to your desired heat level.

For the Marinade

Put the tomatoes, onion, and garlic on a sheet pan with raised sides. Cook them in an oven set at 400°F until the onions soften, about 10 to 20 minutes. Set aside to cool.

Place the roasted vegetables and the remaining marinade ingredients into a blender and process into a thick puree.

Pre-Bath

Preheat the water bath to 131°F / 55°C.

Place the duck legs in a sous vide pouch and pour half the marinade over them. Reserve the rest of the marinade and place in the refrigerator. Seal duck and place in the water bath. Cook for 3 to 6 hours.

Finishing

Remove the duck legs from the sous vide pouches and pat dry. Sear them over high heat on a grill until just browned, about 1 to 2 minutes. Serve with a spoonful of the reserved marinade on top.

HERBED TURKEY BREAST

Time: 1 to 4 Hours
Temperature: 147°F / 63.9°C
Serves: 4

For the Turkey
1-2 pounds turkey breast
1 teaspoon dried thyme
1 teaspoon garlic powder
Salt and pepper

For the Butter
1 stick butter, softened at room temperature
2 tablespoons fresh basil, chopped
1 tablespoon fresh thyme
½ tablespoon fresh oregano, chopped
⅛ teaspoon ground black pepper

*This butter topping adds some great richness to the
normally lean turkey and adds a lot of flavor with the
herbs. You can serve this turkey with a side of rice
and steamed vegetables for a healthy, complete meal.*

Pre-Bath
Preheat the water bath to 147°F / 63.9°C.

Salt and pepper the turkey then sprinkle
with the garlic powder and dried thyme.
Add to the sous vide pouches then seal and
place in the water bath. Cook the turkey for
1 to 4 hours.

Finishing
Heat a grill to high-heat. You won't be
cooking the meat long on it, just searing it,
so use the hottest setting.

To make the butter place all of the butter
ingredients in a bowl and mix and mash
thoroughly using a fork.

Take the turkey out of the pouches and pat
dry. Sear it on a very hot grill for 1 to 2
minutes per side. Place the turkey on a plate
and place a spoonful or two of the butter on
top.

GRILLED TURKEY LEG WITH CRANBERRY BBQ SAUCE

Time: 4 to 8 Hours
Temperature: 145°F / 62.7°C
Serves: 4

For the Turkey
1-2 pounds turkey legs and thighs
1 teaspoon dried thyme
1 teaspoon garlic powder
Salt and pepper

For the BBQ Sauce
1 ½ cups ketchup
3 tablespoons Worcester sauce
¼ cup apple cider vinegar
2 tablespoons yellow mustard
1 tablespoon onion powder
2 tablespoons molasses
⅓ cup cranberry sauce
½ teaspoon mustard powder
Salt and pepper

The cranberry BBQ sauce is a nice twist on a classic Thanksgiving flavor combination. It's great when served with a chunky stuffing or mashed potatoes.

Pre-Bath
Preheat the water bath to 145°F / 62.7°C.

Salt and pepper the turkey then sprinkle with the garlic powder and dried thyme. Add to the sous vide pouches then seal and place in the water bath. Cook the turkey for 4 to 8 hours.

Finishing
Start the BBQ sauce at least 30 to 40 minutes before you want to eat. You can also make it ahead of time and save it in the refrigerator for several months.

Place all of the BBQ sauce ingredients into a pan set over medium-high heat and bring to a boil, stirring regularly to make sure all of the ingredients meld together. Reduce the heat and simmer, stirring regularly, for around 20 minutes until it thickens.

Take the turkey out of the pouches and pat dry. Sear them on a very hot grill for 1 to 2 minutes per side. Place the turkey on a plate and place a spoonful or two of the BBQ sauce on top.

FISH AND SHELLFISH

Cooking Fish and Shellfish

Traditionally fish is often grilled but it can be difficult to use sous vide during this process. Many fish turn light and flaky when cooked and the grilling will just tear them apart.

We've included a few recipes for you but often times fish is best cooked sous vide and served un-browned or just grilled using traditional means.

The FDA states that fish is safe when it is held at 135°F for over 27 minutes, or 140°F for over 8.65 minutes. This is very easy to do with sous vide.

We've found that in general the best tasting seafood is cooked at 132°F. However, unless it is cooked for over 45 minutes it is not fully pasteurized and should not be eaten if you have a weak immune system unless the fish is of sushi-grade quality.

For fully pasteurized fish, it is best to cook them to 140°F. One note is that this will not kill any virus that are in the fish, but this is an issue with traditional methods as well.

Tips and Tricks

Let Them Cool
One way to help the fish to keep from sticking is to let them cool to room temperature before grilling them, or even chilling them in a ½ ice and ½ water bath. This will keep the fish together a little better while you place them on the grill.

Clean and Oil the Grill
To help prevent sticking it is very important that your grill is clean and oiled before placing the fish on. Be sure old food is off the grates then wipe them down with a paper towel or kitchen rag with canola oil on it.

MAHI MAHI WITH CORN SALAD

Time: 10 to 30 Minutes
Temperature: 122°F / 50°C for sushi quality or
132°F / 55.6°C otherwise
Serves: 4

For the Mahi Mahi
4 mahi mahi portions
1 teaspoons garlic powder
½ teaspoon onion powder
½ teaspoon paprika
¼ teaspoon cayenne pepper, or more to taste
Salt and pepper

For the Corn Salad
3 cups corn
½ pint cherry tomatoes, halved
1 red bell pepper, diced
2 tablespoons fresh basil, chopped

For the Dressing
2 tablespoons lime juice
1 teaspoon ancho chile powder
1 tablespoon olive oil
Salt and pepper

1 tablespoon fresh basil, chopped, for garnish
1 lime, quartered, for garnish

*Mahi Mahi is a full flavored fish that can stand up to
bolder ingredients. Here we pair it with some summer
vegetables and a lime vinaigrette with some moderate
heat. For a spicier dish you can add sliced serrano or
jalapeno peppers to the dressing. For some extra
grilled flavor you can half the lime and grill it for a
few minutes until it caramelizes slightly.*

Pre Bath
Preheat the water bath to the indicated
temperature.

Salt and pepper each mahi mahi filet. Mix
together the garlic powder, onion powder,
paprika, and cayenne together. Sprinkle the
spice mixture on top of the fish, add to the
sous vide pouches, and seal. Place into the
water bath and cook for 10 to 30 minutes.

Finishing
Preheat the oven to 400°F.

Place the corn kernels and red pepper on a
baking tray with raised edges. Drizzle olive
oil over the top and salt and pepper. Cook
until the kernels are soft, 5 to 10 minutes.

In a large bowl, combine the roasted corn,
tomatoes, roasted red pepper and basil and
mix well. In a small bowl whisk together the
ingredients for the dressing and pour over
the corn.

Preheat a grill to high heat.

Take the mahi mahi out of the pouch and
pat dry. Sear over high-heat on a hot grill,
about 1 to 2 minutes per side.

To serve, take a large spoonful of the corn
mixture and place on individual plates.
Place the mahi-mahi on top. Top with a lime
wedge and the basil and serve.

LEMON-TARRAGON SWORDFISH

Time: 15 to 30 Minutes
Temperature: 132°F / 55.5°C
Serves: 2

For the Swordfish
2 swordfish portions
1 tablespoon butter
Salt and pepper

For the Butter
½ stick butter, softened at room temperature
2 tablespoons fresh tarragon, finely chopped
1 teaspoon grated lemon zest
⅛ teaspoon ground black pepper

The flavor of the swordfish is brightened by the lemon-tarragon butter and it is also a very quick and easy dish to make. This dish is great with steamed vegetables or a light risotto.

Pre-Bath
Preheat the water bath to 132°F / 55.5°C.

Salt and pepper the swordfish then add to the sous vide pouches. Add the butter and then seal and place in the water bath. Cook the swordfish for 15 to 30 minutes.

Finishing
Preheat a grill to high heat.

To make the butter place all of the butter ingredients in a bowl and mix and mash thoroughly using a fork.

Take the swordfish out of the pouch and pat dry. Sear it on a very hot grill for 1 to 2 minutes per side. Place the swordfish on a plate and place a dollop or two of the butter on top.

MAHI MAHI WITH CHIPOTLE BUTTER

Time: 10 to 30 Minutes
Temperature: 122°F / 50°C for sushi quality or
132°F / 55.6°C otherwise
Serves: 4

For the Mahi Mahi
4 portions of mahi mahi, 1-2 pounds
½ teaspoon paprika
½ teaspoon cumin
Salt and pepper

For the Butter
½ stick butter, softened at room temperature
¼-1 teaspoon chipotle puree
½ teaspoon cumin
⅛ teaspoon ground black pepper

The flavor of the mahi mahi is deepened and enhanced by this hot and smoky butter. You can add more or less of the chipotle peppers to get to the hotness you prefer. To make the chipotle puree simply process a can of chipotle peppers in adobo sauce in a blender or food processor until smooth. This dish is great with roasted root vegetables.

Pre-Bath

Preheat the water bath to the indicated temperature.

Salt and pepper the mahi mahi then sprinkle with the paprika and cumin. Place in the sous vide pouches, seal, and place in the water bath. Cook the mahi mahi for 10 to 30 minutes.

Finishing

Preheat a grill to high heat.

To make the butter place all of the butter ingredients in a bowl and mix and mash thoroughly using a fork.

Take the mahi mahi out of the pouches and pat dry. Sear it on a very hot grill for 1 to 2 minutes per side. Place the mahi mahi on a plate and place a dollop or two of the butter on top.

SEA BASS WITH HERB SALAD

Time: 15 to 30 Minutes
Temperature: 122°F / 50°C for sushi quality,
otherwise 132°F / 55.5°C
Serves: 2

For the Sea Bass
2 portions of sea bass
2 tablespoons butter
Salt and pepper

For the Herb Salad
1 cup mixed soft herbs like basil, oregano,
    parsley, tarragon, chives, mint and chervil
1 cup frisée lettuce, coarsely chopped
1 lemon
1 tablespoon olive oil
Salt and pepper

*The strong flavor of the herb salad helps to spruce up
the sea bass. This herb salad is great with many
different kinds of fish and can even be used with a
fattier cut of steak like a ribeye. This dish is great
when served with a side of roasted potatoes or a hearty
risotto.*

Pre-Bath

Preheat the water bath to the indicated
temperature.

Season the sea bass with the salt and pepper
then add to the sous vide pouch. Add the
butter to the pouch and then seal. Place in
the water bath and cook for 15 to 30
minutes.

Finishing

Preheat a grill to high heat.

Take the sea bass out of the pouch, reserving
the butter liquid. Pat dry the sea bass and
sear one side over high-heat on a hot grill
for 1 to 2 minutes.

Place the sea bass on the plates with the
grilled side up and top with the herbs and
frisée. Sprinkle with salt and pepper. Spoon
some of the juices from the sous vide pouch
on the greens. Drizzle the olive oil over top
and squeeze the lemon equally over the two
portions.

COD WITH SPICY BEAN SALAD

Time: 10 to 30 Minutes
Temperature: 129°F / 53.9°C for sushi quality or
132°F / 55.6°C otherwise
Serves: 4

For the Cod
4 cod portions
½ teaspoon ground cumin
2 tablespoons butter or olive oil
Salt and pepper

For the Salad
1 15-ounce can black beans, drained and washed
1 15-ounce can pinto beans, drained and washed
2 cups corn kernels
1 orange or red bell pepper, diced
1 poblano pepper, diced
1 shallot, diced
¼ cup red onion, finely diced
¼ cup fresh cilantro, chopped

For the Vinaigrette
½ teaspoon ground cumin
½ teaspoon ancho chile powder
⅛ teaspoon cayenne powder
6 tablespoons fresh lime juice
5 tablespoons olive oil
½ teaspoon salt
½ teaspoon black pepper

*Often times cod is a blander fish. We try to spice it up
here with a hearty bean salad with a spicy vinaigrette.
We recommend ancho chile powder and poblano
peppers but you can use any type of chile powder or
hot pepper that you prefer.*

Pre Bath

Preheat the water bath to the indicated
temperature.

Salt and pepper each cod portion, sprinkle
with the ground cumin, and add to the sous
vide pouches. Add the butter or olive oil
and seal. Place into the water bath and cook
for 10 to 30 minutes.

Finishing

Cook the corn, peppers, and onion in a
350°F oven for 5 to 10 minutes.

Prepare the vinaigrette in a small bowl by
combining the spices, lime juice, salt, and
pepper. Slowly whisk in the olive oil.

In a large bowl combine the beans, corn,
peppers, onion, shallot, and cilantro. Add
enough vinaigrette to thoroughly coat the
salad.

Take the cod out of the pouches and pat dry.
Sear one side over high heat on a grill just
until browned, one to two minutes. Remove
from the heat.

To serve get 4 plates. On each plate put a
spoonful of the salad with the cod, seared
side up, resting on the top.

HADDOCK WITH HERB VINAIGRETTE

Time: 15 to 30 Minutes
Temperature: 122°F / 50°C for sushi quality,
otherwise 132°F / 55.5°C
Serves: 4

For the Haddock
1 ½ pounds of haddock, cut in 4 portions
1 tablespoon butter
Salt and pepper

For the Vinaigrette
2 tablespoons white wine vinegar
½ tablespoon shallot, minced
1 garlic clove, minced
Salt and pepper
6 tablespoons olive oil
¼ cup fresh basil, chopped
¼ cup fresh parsley, chopped

*This recipe is very good with any white, mild fish. You
can also play around with the herbs in the vinaigrette,
mix and matching to your preference. Combined with
steamed vegetables this dish makes a nice, light meal.*

Pre-Bath

Preheat the water bath to the indicated
temperature.

Season the haddock with the salt and
pepper. Add to the sous vide pouch along
with the butter and seal. Place the sous vide
pouch into the water bath and cook for 15 to
30 minutes.

Finishing

First, make the vinaigrette. Combine the
vinegar, shallot, garlic, salt, and pepper in a
small bowl. Let sit for 5 minutes. Slowly
whisk in the olive oil then stir in the herbs.

Take the haddock out of the sous vide
pouches and pat dry. Sear it over high-heat
on a hot grill until just browned, about 1
minute per side.

Serve the haddock with the vinaigrette
spooned over it.

GRILLED LOBSTER

Time: 15 to 35 Minutes
Temperature: 126°F / 52.2°C for sushi quality or
140°F / 60°C otherwise
Serves: 4

4 lobster tails, split
6 tablespoons butter
4 thyme sprigs
4 lemon wedges
1 tablespoon fresh tarragon, chopped
2-4 ounces butter, melted

*Grilled lobster is a great meal to make during the
summer. It's nice and light and goes great with grilled
corn on the cob, clam chowder, and french fries. The
lobsters can be cooked with sous vide ahead of time,
quickly chilled, and them held until you are ready to
grill them.*

Pre-Bath

Preheat the water bath to 126°F / 52.2°C for
sushi quality or 140°F / 60°C otherwise.

Place the lobster tails, the butter, and the
thyme sprigs in the sous vide pouches.
Sprinkle with salt and pepper then seal the
pouches and place in the water bath to cook
for 15 to 35 minutes.

Finishing

Heat a grill to high heat.

Remove the lobster tails from the sous vide
pouches and pat dry. Place them flesh side
down on the grill and cook until they begin
to brown, about 2 minutes.

Serve the lobster with the lemon wedges
and a bowl of the warm, melted butter with
the tarragon mixed in so people can dip the
lobster while they are eating.

LAMB

COOKING LAMB

Lamb is not as commonly cooked on the grill as some of the other food types. However, some of the most impressive results of sous vide are created with tough cuts of lamb. We have several recipes for lamb chops, which are the most commonly grilled item, and also a few recipes for leg of lamb and loin roasts.

Sous vide allows you to do things that traditional methods are unable to accomplish, such as cooking the roasts medium-rare and falling apart tender. This allows you to pre-cook the lamb using sous vide and then finish it off on the grill for extra flavor.

We recommend cooking medium-rare lamb at 131°F / 55°C to give yourself a few degrees of temperature variation above the bottom of the safe zone. If you prefer medium lamb we recommend not going above 140°F / 60°C because the lamb begins drying out quickly and with sous vide there is no gain in food safety above 131°F / 55°C. But feel free to experiment with any temperatures in that range.

TIPS AND TRICKS

Take Advantage of the Tough Cuts

Cooking a roast or leg of lamb with sous vide first and then finishing it on the grill is a great way to take advantage of tough cuts. These cuts are usually very flavorful and also look quite impressive when you take them off the grill.

ROSEMARY MUSTARD LAMB CHOPS

Time: 2 to 4 Hours
Temperature: 131°F / 55°C
Serves: 4

8-10 lamb chops

For the Rub
1 tablespoon whole yellow mustard seeds
¼ cup garlic, minced
6-8 rosemary sprigs, chopped
2 tablespoons Worcester sauce
2 tablespoons olive oil
2 tablespoons coarse salt (kosher or sea)
1 tablespoon dark brown sugar
2 teaspoons mustard powder
1 tablespoon cracked black pepper

This dish features a bold rosemary-mustard rub for the lamb chops that helps to bring out the natural flavors of the lamb.

For the Rub

Grind the mustard seeds in a spice grinder or place them in a ziploc bag and crack them by rolling over them with a rolling pin. Place the mustard seeds and remaining ingredients into a bowl and mix together.

Pre-Bath

Preheat the water bath to 131°F / 55°C.

Rub the rosemary-mustard paste all over the lamb chops. Place the lamb chops in the sous vide pouches and seal. Any excess paste can be refrigerated for about a week. Place the sous vide pouches into the water and cook for 2 to 4 hours.

Finishing

Heat a grill to high-heat. You won't be cooking the meat long on it, just searing it, so use the hottest setting.

Take the lamb chops out of the sous vide bath and pat dry. On a very hot grill sear the lamb chops, 1 to 2 minutes per side. Remove from the heat and serve.

LAMB CHOPS WITH MELON RELISH

Time: 2 to 4 Hours
Temperature: 131°F / 55°C
Serves: 4

For the Lamb
8 lamb chops
1 teaspoon dried thyme
1 teaspoon garlic powder
Salt and pepper

For the Relish
¼ cup lime juice
2 tablespoons brown sugar
1 tablespoon fresh ginger, minced
½ teaspoon ground cinnamon
2 cups watermelon, diced
2 cups cantaloup or honeydew, diced
1 cucumber, peeled, seeded, and diced
½ cup red onion, diced
1-3 jalapeno chilies, seeded and diced
⅓ cup fresh mint, chopped

The relish in this dish features chunks of melon and cucumber which help to bring out the sweetness in the lamb and has a little heat from the jalapeno peppers for added bite.

Pre-Bath

Preheat the water bath to 131°F / 55°C.

Mix together the dried thyme, garlic powder, salt and pepper and sprinkle over the lamb chops. Place the lamb chops in the sous vide pouches and seal. Place the sous vide pouches into the water bath and cook for 2 to 4 hours.

Finishing

Up to 30 minutes before the lamb is done make the relish. Whisk the lime juice, brown sugar, ginger, and cinnamon in a bowl until the sugar is dissolved. Add the remaining ingredients and mix well.

Take the lamb chops out of the sous vide bath and pat dry. On a very hot grill sear the lamb chops, 1 to 2 minutes per side.

Serve the lamb chops with a spoonful or two of the relish on top.

SPICED LEG OF LAMB

Time: 2 to 3 Days
Temperature: 131°F / 55°C
Serves: 4

1 pound lamb leg

For the Marinade
½ cup olive oil
¼ cup fresh oregano, coarsely chopped
¼ cup lemon juice
¼ cup fresh basil, coarsely chopped
5 garlic cloves, coarsely chopped
1 tablespoon chipotle puree
½ teaspoon black pepper
½ teaspoon salt

This leg of lamb has a nice garlic bite to it along with the heat from the pepper flakes. It is good when featured alongside a hearty risotto or mashed potatoes.

You can also take the juice from the sous vide pouch and make a gravy with it, adding some veal or chicken stock if needed.

For the Marinade
Whisk together the lemon juice, pepper, chipotle puree, and salt in a bowl until the salt is dissolved. Add the garlic, oregano, and basil and whisk in the olive oil. Cover the lamb leg with the marinade and refrigerate for 8 to 12 hours.

Pre-Bath
Preheat the water bath to 131°F / 55°C.

Remove the lamb from the marinade and place it in a sous vide pouch. Sprinkle with salt and pepper and seal the pouch. Place the pouch in the water bath and cook for 2 to 3 days.

Finishing
Heat a grill to high-heat. You won't be cooking the meat long on it, just searing it, so use the hottest setting.

Remove the lamb from the water bath and sous vide pouch. Pat it dry and sear over high heat on a grill until browned, 1 to 2 minutes per side. Slice the lamb into portions and serve.

GRILLED RACK OF LAMB

Time: 2 to 3 Hours
Temperature: 131°F / 55°C
Serves: 4

2 1-pound racks of lamb, frenched
4 rosemary sprigs
8 thyme sprigs
2 tablespoons butter or olive oil
Salt and pepper

This rack of lamb is very rustic and simple. It looks very impressive on the grill and tastes great.

It's goes well with homestyle mashed potatoes and grilled vegetables.

Pre-Bath

Preheat the water bath to 131°F / 55°C.

Place the lamb in a sous vide pouch with the rosemary, thyme, and butter. Sprinkle with salt and pepper and seal the pouch. Place the pouch in the water bath and cook for 2 to 3 hours.

Finishing

Remove the lamb from the water bath and sous vide pouches, reserving the liquid from the pouches. Pat the lamb dry.

Sear the lamb over high heat on a grill until browned, 1 to 2 minutes per side. Remove from the heat and cut the lamb into serving portions.

Serve the lamb with the reserved juices spooned on top or in a small dish on the side.

LAMB CHOPS WITH HARISSA

Time: 2 to 4 Hours
Temperature: 131°F / 55°C
Serves: 4 to 6

For the Lamb
12 lamb chops
1 teaspoon ground cumin
1 teaspoon ground coriander
Salt and pepper

For the Harissa
1 teaspoon ground cumin
1 teaspoon caraway seeds
1 large roasted red bell pepper, coarsely chopped
2 garlic cloves, coarsely chopped
2 small hot red chiles, coarsely chopped
1 teaspoon kosher salt
3 tablespoons olive oil
¼ cup cilantro, chopped
Juice of 1 lemon
4 tablespoons olive oil
Salt and pepper

Harissa is a hot chile sauce often eaten in North Africa. Here we use it to add bold flavors to the lamb chops.

Pre-Bath
Preheat the water bath to 131°F / 55°C.

Sprinkle the lamb chops with the cumin and coriander then salt and pepper them. Add to the sous vide pouches and seal. Place the pouches in the water bath and cook for 2 to 4 hours.

For the Harissa
Put all ingredients into a blender or food processor and process until pureed well. This can be stored in the refrigerator for several weeks.

Finishing
Heat a grill to high-heat. You won't be cooking the meat long on it, just searing it, so use the hottest setting.

Take the lamb chops out of the sous vide bath and pat dry. On a very hot grill sear the lamb chops, 1 to 2 minutes per side.

Serve the lamb chops with the harissa sauce spooned on top or in small bowls on the side.

TURKISH LOIN ROAST

Time: 2 to 4 Hours
Temperature: 131°F / 55°C
Serves: 4 to 6

2-3 pounds lamb loin

For the Marinade
2 cups plain whole milk yogurt
½ cup olive oil
3 tablespoons lemon juice
1 onion, chopped
3 garlic cloves, minced
1 teaspoon salt
½ teaspoon black pepper
½ teaspoon hot pepper flakes

This marinade helps add a lot of flavor to the lamb loin. The yogurt also helps to slightly change the meat, making it more tender. The lamb is very good when served with some creamy polenta or rustic mashed potatoes.

For the Marinade
Place the yogurt in a bowl and mix in the rest of the marinade ingredients.

Cover the lamb loin with the marinade and refrigerate for 6 to 12 hours.

Pre-Bath
Preheat the water bath to 131°F / 55°C for medium-rare.

Remove the lamb from the marinade and place it in the sous vide pouch and seal. Place the pouch in the water bath and cook for 2 to 4 hours.

Finishing
Heat a grill to high-heat. You won't be cooking the meat long on it, just searing it, so use the hottest setting.

Take the lamb loin out of the sous vide bath and pat dry. On a very hot grill sear the lamb, 1 to 2 minutes per side. Remove from the heat and serve.

LEMON-MINT LAMB CHOPS

Time: 2 to 4 Hours
Temperature: 131°F / 55°C
Serves: 4 to 6

For the Lamb
12 lamb chops
1 teaspoon ground cumin
1 paprika powder
Salt and pepper

For the Butter
½ stick butter, softened at room temperature
2 tablespoons fresh mint, finely chopped
1 garlic clove, finely minced
¼ teaspoon lemon zest, grated
⅛ teaspoon ground black pepper

The flavor of the lamb is brightened by this citrusy butter. The butter is quick to put together and very simple. This dish is great with steamed vegetables and rice.

Pre-Bath

Preheat the water bath to 131°F / 55°C.

Salt and pepper the lamb chops then sprinkle with the cumin and paprika. Add to the sous vide pouches and then seal. Place in the water bath and cook for 2 to 4 hours.

Finishing

To make the butter place all of the butter ingredients in a bowl and mix and mash thoroughly using a fork.

Take the lamb chops out of the sous vide bath and pat dry. On a very hot grill sear the lamb chops, 1 to 2 minutes per side.

Place the lamb chops on a plate and place a spoonful or two of the butter on top.

Brazilian Lamb Chops

Time: 2 to 4 Hours
Temperature: 131°F / 55°C
Serves: 4 to 6

12 lamb chops

For the Marinade
6 garlic cloves, coarsely chopped
2 teaspoons salt
¼ cup lime juice
¼ cup white wine
1 tablespoon red wine vinegar
2 teaspoons hot sauce
3 tablespoons fresh parsley, coarsely chopped
1 tablespoon fresh rosemary, coarsely chopped
1 tablespoon fresh mint, coarsely chopped

Using this marinade before cooking the lamb chops deeply flavors the meat and adds moisture to the inside of the lamb. The lamb is great when served with a bold risotto or a salad of mixed greens.

For the Marinade

Place all of the marinade ingredients into a blender and pulse several times until mixed well. Cover the lamb chops with the marinade and refrigerate for 2 to 4 hours.

Pre-Bath

Preheat the water bath to 131°F / 55°C.

Remove the lamb chops from the marinade and place them in the sous vide pouches and seal. Place the pouches in the water bath and cook for 2 to 4 hours.

Finishing

Take the lamb chops out of the sous vide bath and pat dry. On a very hot grill sear the lamb chops, 1 to 2 minutes per side. Remove from the heat and serve.

Pork

COOKING PORK

Pork is probably used in BBQ more than in grilling but with sous vide you can have some amazing results.

There are two main benefits to cooking pork with sous vide. The first is that sous vide allows you to safely cook pork to medium-rare doneness. The other benefit is the ability to tenderize tougher cuts of pork through longer cooking times without drying them out.

We recommend cooking medium-rare pork at 135°F / 57°C to give yourself a few degrees of temperature variation above the bottom of the safe zone. If you prefer medium pork we recommend not going above 140°F / 60°C because the lamb begins drying out quickly and with sous vide there is no gain in food safety above 131°F / 55°C. But feel free to experiment with any temperatures in that range.

TIPS AND TRICKS

Go for the Lean

Unless you are planning on making pulled pork or another similar type of dish it is normally best to stick to the leaner cuts of pork. The fat doesn't break down as well during the sous vide process and since you are finishing on the grill it won't have a lot of time to break down afterwards.

The sous vide process will keep the meat nice and moist so even leaner cuts will work great. I really enjoy pork chops and pork loins.

Brining for Flavor

If you want to introduce extra flavor and moisture to your pork then brining the meat ahead of time is a great idea. The brine will help to infuse the meat with flavor and keep them even more moist than normal.

SMOKY PORK TENDERLOIN

Time: 3 to 6 Hours
Temperature: 135°F / 57.2°C
Serves: 4 to 6

For the Rub
1 tablespoon ground coriander
1 tablespoon ground cumin
1 tablespoon garlic powder
1 tablespoon paprika
2 teaspoons mustard powder
1 teaspoon chipotle powder
Salt and pepper

For the Pork
3 pounds pork tenderloin

Grilling a whole pork tenderloin results in a dramatic presentation. Using sous vide to first cook the pork through ensures you will have a perfectly cooked piece of meat. Finishing it on the grill, in addition to the paprika and chipotle, adds a good amount of smokiness and grill flavor.

Pre-Bath

Preheat the water bath to 135°F / 57.2°C.

Mix the spices together in a bowl. Salt and pepper the pork loin, then coat with the spices. Place it in the pouch and seal. Place in the water bath and cook for 3 to 6 hours.

Finishing

Heat a grill to high-heat. You won't be cooking the meat long on it, just searing it, so use the hottest setting.

Remove the pork from the sous vide pouch and pat dry. Salt and pepper the pork then sear on a grill over high heat until just charred. Remove from the heat and slice on the bias.

You can also drizzle some of the juices from the pouch over the sliced pork to act as a sauce.

JAMAICAN PORK CHOPS

Time: 3 to 6 Hours
Temperature: 135°F / 57.2°C
Serves: 4

4 pork chops
⅓ cup dark brown sugar
¼ cup salt
1 tablespoon black pepper
1 tablespoon garlic powder
1 tablespoon onion powder
1-3 teaspoons scotch bonnet or habanero chile
   powder
2 teaspoons dried thyme
1 teaspoon ground coriander
1 teaspoon ground allspice
1 teaspoon cumin
½ teaspoon dried ginger
½ teaspoon ground cinnamon
¼ teaspoon ground cloves
¼ teaspoon ground nutmeg

*This recipe is great when served with traditional
Jamaican side dishes such as mashed or fried
plantains and rice and peas. The heat from the rub
really helps to spice up pork chops and other blander
cuts like chicken breast or pork tenderloin.*

Pre-Bath
Preheat the water bath to 135°F / 57.2°C.

First make the Jamaican rub by combining
all of the ingredients except the pork chops
in a bowl and mixing well.

Sprinkle the rub over the pork chops and
place them in the sous vide pouches. Seal
the pouches then place in the water bath
and cook for 3 to 6 hours.

Finishing
Heat a grill to high-heat. You won't be
cooking the meat long on it, just searing it,
so use the hottest setting.

Remove the pork chops from their pouches
and pat them dry. Quickly sear them on
both sides on a grill over high heat, about 1
or 2 minutes per side. Remove from the heat
and serve.

HERB BRINED PORK LOIN

Time: 4 to 8 Hours
Temperature: 135°F / 57.2°C
Serves: 4 to 6

For the Brine
2 bay leaves
1 onion, roughly chopped
2 carrots, roughly chopped
1 tablespoon peppercorns
1 tablespoon whole coriander
4 rosemary sprigs
4 thyme sprigs
Enough water to cover your meat
¾ teaspoon salt per cup of water

For the Pork
2 pounds pork loin
1 rosemary sprig
2 thyme sprigs

*Using the brine in this recipe really infuses the loin
with tons of flavor. You can change around the
ingredients for the brine as long as the salt to water
ratio stays about the same.*

*You can use this same brining process with chicken
breasts.*

Brining

Combine all of the brining ingredients into a
pot and heat on the stove until it comes to a
boil, stirring occasionally. Stir the brine well
to make sure all of the salt is dissolved then
turn the heat down and let simmer for at
least 10 minutes.

Remove the brine from the heat and cool it
off completely.

Place the meat into the brine. It should be
completely submerged under the brine.
Refrigerate the meat in the brine for 4 to 12
hours, depending on the thickness of it.

Pre-Bath

Preheat the water bath to 135°F / 57.2°C.

Remove the pork loin from the brine, place
in a sous vide pouch and seal. Place in the
water bath and cook for 4 to 8 hours.

Finishing

Remove the pork from the sous vide pouch
and pat dry. Salt and pepper the pork then
sear on a grill over high heat until just
charred.

Remove from the heat and slice on the bias.
Serve with some olive oil drizzled over the
top.

CHINESE 5 SPICE PORK CHOP

Time: 4 to 8 Hours
Temperature: 135°F / 57.2°C
Serves: 4

4 pork chops
1 tablespoon soy sauce
2 tablespoons Chinese 5 spice powder
1 tablespoon Worcester sauce
Salt and pepper

This is a super simple meal to put together. Using pre-mixed spice mixes like this is a great way to cut down on your prep time and add a lot of variety to your meals.

Chinese 5 spice powder adds a lot of great flavor to food. These pork chops are even better when served with some fried rice.

Pre-Bath

Preheat the water bath to 135°F / 57.2°C.

Lightly salt and pepper the pork chops and sprinkle with the Chinese 5 spice powder. Place the pork chops in the sous vide pouches and add the soy sauce and Worcester sauce. Seal the sous vide pouches, place in the water bath, and cook for 4 to 8 hours.

Finishing

Heat a grill to high-heat. You won't be cooking the meat long on it, just searing it, so use the hottest setting.

Remove the pork chops from their pouches and pat dry. Quickly sear the pork chops on both sides on a grill, about 1 or 2 minutes per side. Remove from the heat and serve.

PORK LOIN WITH OLIVE TAPENADE

Time: 4 to 8 Hours
Temperature: 135°F / 57.2°C
Serves: 4

For the Pork
1-2 pounds pork loin roast
1 teaspoon garlic powder
1 teaspoon paprika
½ teaspoon cumin
Salt and pepper

For the Olive Tapenade
1 cup kalamata olives, pitted
2 anchovy filets or 1 tablespoon capers
2 garlic cloves
¼ teaspoon red pepper flakes
1 tablespoon fresh parsley, chopped
2 tablespoons balsamic or red wine vinegar
3 tablespoons olive oil
Salt and pepper

The saltiness of the olives and anchovies helps bring out the flavor of the pork. This dish is great when served with roasted tomatoes or vegetables, or even a crisp salad. This tapenade is also very good with steak or lamb.

Pre-Bath

Preheat the water bath to 135°F / 57.2°C.

In a bowl mix together the garlic powder, paprika and cumin. Salt and pepper the pork and then sprinkle the spice mix over top. Add to the sous vide pouch and seal. Place in the water bath and cook for 4 to 8 hours.

Finishing

About 5 minutes before the pork is done make the olive tapenade. Put all of the tapenade ingredients into a food processor and pulse several times until it forms a coarse puree.

Remove the pork from the water bath and pat dry. Sear the pork on a very hot grill for 1 to 2 minutes per side. Remove from the heat and place on a plate. Spoon the tapenade across the top of the pork loin and serve.

Time and Temperature Charts

You can also get this time and temperature information
on your mobile phone if you have an iPhone, iPad or an Android.

Just search for "Sous Vide" and look for the guide by "Primolicious".

One of the most interesting aspects of sous vide cooking is how much the time and temperature used can change the texture of the food. Many people experiment with different cooking times and temperatures to tweak dishes various ways.

The numbers below are merely beginning recommendations and are a good place to start. Feel free to increase or lower the temperature several degrees or play around with the cooking time as you see fit as long as you stay in the safe-zone.

DONENESS RANGE

One of the most common questions we get asked about our sous vide recipes is some variation of "the recipe says to cook it for 3 to 6 hours, but when is it actually done".

The short answer is that anytime within the given range the food is "done". As long as the food has been in the waterbath for more than the minimum time and less than the maximum time, then it is done. There isn't a specific magical moment of true doneness that can be generalized.

For those that want more information, here's the explanation why.

The How and Why

To have this conversation we first need to determine what "done" actually means. For sous vide there are two main "doneness" concerns when cooking your food. The first is to ensure that the food actually comes up to the temperature you are cooking it at (or becomes pasteurized at for some food). The second concern is making sure the food is tender enough to eat without being "over tender", mushy, or dry.

Once the food you are cooking is completely up to temperature and it is tenderized enough to eat (and not over tenderized), it is now "done". For some already tender cuts of meat like filets, loins, and chicken breasts you don't have to worry about tenderness since they start out that way. That means that these cuts are "done" once they get up to temperature. You can find out this time using our Sous Vide Thickness Ruler.

However, despite them being "done" at the minimum time shown, they stay "done" for several hours past that time, depending on the starting tenderness of the meat. This is why we give a range. You can eat a 1" cut of filet mignon after 50 minutes but you can also eat the filet up to 3 hours after it has gone into the bath without any loss in quality, tenderness, or flavor.

This is how our ranges are determined. They specify that for an average cut of the given meat, they will become "great to eat" tender at the minimum time given. They will continue to get more tender the longer they are in the bath but will remain "great to eat" tender until the final time given, at which point they may begin to get mushy and overcooked. In essence, they will be "done", and very tasty, for that entire span between the minimum and maximum times.

Another Way to Look at It

Another way to think about how this works is to use the following analogy. Pretend you were helping a new cook grill a steak. If they told you they wanted to cook it medium rare and asked you to tell them how to tell when it was "done", what would you say?

Most people would reply with "when the temperature is between 131°F to 139°F".

If the friend isn't a cook they would ask "Yeah, but when is it actually done?"

The answer at this point really comes down to personal preference since to some people medium-rare is perfect at 131°F and others prefer a little more well-done 135°F, but a medium-rare steak is "done" anywhere in that range.

Other Critical Variables

One other complicating factor is that there are many variables that go into determining how fast a piece of meat tenderizes and/or becomes tender.

The most obvious variable is that some cuts of meat are tougher than others. For example, a top round roast needs to be tenderized a lot longer than a ribeye. Most people realize this and that's why almost all sous vide charts break the food down by "cut".

Another less obvious but almost as important factor is where the meat came from. There is a big difference between how fast the meat tenderizes and how the cow was raised. I've found that grass-fed meat from my local farmer needs just 1/2 the time to become tender compared to supermarket meat (this is also true when roasting or braising them). I've also talked to a reader in Mexico who eats local grass-fed beef that needs slightly longer times than normal because the cows work more.

There are then the variables in the actual cow itself. Whether the meat is prime, choice, etc. makes a difference in tenderizing time. As does the marbling, how old the meat is, and several other factors.

So taking all of this together it can be hard to accurately determine a range of "doneness" that will work for all cuts of meat. But we try our best to come up with a nice range of times that the "average" piece of meat will be done in. The only way to really learn is to experiment with the types of meat in your area and see how they react. And luckily for us, sous vide allows us to have a wide range that food is done in.

In Conclusion

So while there might be one magical moment in the cooking process where a certain piece of meat is the most ideal tenderness, in practice there is a wide time range in the cooking process where the meat will be "done". As long as you take it out sometime in that range it should turn out great.

As you get more experience with your local meats, and determine your personal preferences, you can start to tweak your cook times to suit them more exactly. But as you are learning just remember that the food will be "done" anywhere in that range, and don't sweat the details!

Beef Roasts and Tough Cuts

Bottom Round Roast

Medium Rare	131°F for 2 to 3 Days (55.0°C)
Medium	140°F for 2 to 3 Days (60.0°C)
Well-Traditional	160°F for 1 to 2 Days (71.1°C)

Brisket

Medium Rare	131°F for 2 to 3 Days (55.0°C)
Medium	140°F for 2 to 3 Days (60.0°C)
Well-Traditional	160°F for 1 to 2 Days (71.1°C)

Cheek

Medium Rare	131°F for 2 to 3 Days (55.0°C)
Medium	149°F for 2 to 3 Days (65.0°C)
Well-Traditional	160°F for 1 to 2 Days (71.1°C)

Chuck Roast

Medium Rare	131°F for 2 to 3 Days (55.0°C)
Medium	140°F for 2 to 3 Days (60.0°C)
Well-Traditional	160°F for 1 to 2 Days (71.1°C)

Pot Roast

Medium Rare	131°F for 2 to 3 Days (55.0°C)
Medium	140°F for 2 to 3 Days (60.0°C)
Well-Traditional	160°F for 1 to 2 Days (71.1°C)

Prime Rib Roast

Medium Rare	131°F for 5 to 10 Hours (55°C)
Medium	140°F for 5 to 10 Hours (60°C)

Rib Eye Roast

Medium Rare	131°F for 5 to 10 Hours (55°C)
Medium	140°F for 5 to 10 Hours (60°C)

Ribs

Medium Rare	131°F for 2 to 3 Days (55.0°C)
Medium	140°F for 2 to 3 Days (60.0°C)
Well-Traditional	160°F for 1 to 2 Days (71.1°C)

Shank

Medium Rare	131°F for 2 to 3 Days (55.0°C)
Medium	140°F for 2 to 3 Days (60.0°C)
Well-Traditional	160°F for 1 to 2 Days (71.1°C)

Short Ribs

Medium Rare	131°F for 2 to 3 Days (55.0°C)
Medium	140°F for 2 to 3 Days (60.0°C)
Well-Traditional	160°F for 1 to 2 Days (71.1°C)

Sirloin Roast

Medium Rare	131°F for 5 to 10 Hours (55.0°C)
Medium	140°F for 5 to 10 Hours (60.0°C)

Stew Meat

Medium Rare	131°F for 4 to 8 Hours (55.0°C)
Medium	140°F for 4 to 8 Hours (60.0°C)

Sweetbreads

Medium	140°F for 30 to 45 Min (60°C)
Pre-Roasting	152°F for 60 Min (66.7°C)

Tenderloin Roast

Medium Rare	131°F for 3 to 6 Hours (55.0°C)
Medium	140°F for 3 to 6 Hours (60.0°C)

Tongue

Low and Slow	140°F for 48 Hours (60.0°C)
High and Fast	158°F for 24 Hours (70.0°C)

Top Loin Strip Roast

Medium Rare	131°F for 4 to 8 Hours (55.0°C)
Medium	140°F for 4 to 8 Hours (60.0°C)

Top Round Roast

Medium Rare	131°F for 1 to 3 Days (55.0°C)
Medium	140°F for 1 to 3 Days (60.0°C)
Well-Traditional	160°F for 1 to 2 Days (71.1°C)

Tri-Tip Roast

Medium Rare	131°F for 5 to 10 Hours (55°C)
Medium	140°F for 5 to 10 Hours (60°C)

Beef - Steak and Tender Cuts

Blade Steak

Medium Rare	131°F for 4 to 10 Hours (55.0°C)
Medium	140°F for 4 to 10 Hours (60.0°C)

Bottom Round Steak

Medium Rare	131°F for 1 to 3 Days (55.0°C)
Medium	140°F for 1 to 3 Days (60.0°C)

Chuck Steak

Medium Rare	131°F for 1 to 2 Days (55.0°C)
Medium	140°F for 1 to 2 Days (60.0°C)

Eye Round Steak

Medium Rare	131°F for 1 to 2 Days (55.0°C)
Medium	140°F for 1 to 2 Days (60.0°C)

Flank Steak

Medium Rare	131°F for 2 to 12 Hours (55.0°C)
Medium Rare and Tender	131°F for 1 to 2 Days (55.0°C)
Medium	140°F for 2 to 12 Hours (60.0°C)
Medium and Tender	140°F for 1 to 2 Days (60.0°C)

Flat Iron Steak

Medium Rare	131°F for 4 to 10 Hours (55.0°C)
Medium	140°F for 4 to 10 Hours (60.0°C)

Hamburger

Medium Rare	131°F for 2 to 4 Hours (55.0°C)
Medium	140°F for 2 to 4 Hours (60.0°C)

Hanger Steak

Medium Rare	131°F for 2 to 3 Hours (55.0°C)
Medium	140°F for 2 to 3 Hours (60.0°C)

Porterhouse Steak

Medium Rare	131°F for 2 to 3 Hours (55.0°C)
Medium	140°F for 2 to 3 Hours (60.0°C)

Rib Steak

Medium Rare	131°F for 2 to 8 Hours (55.0°C)
Medium	140°F for 2 to 8 Hours (60.0°C)

Ribeye Steak

Medium Rare	131°F for 2 to 8 Hours (55.0°C)
Medium	140°F for 2 to 8 Hours (60.0°C)

Sausage

Medium Rare	131°F for 2 to 3 Hours (55.0°C)
Medium	140°F for 90 to 120 Min (60.0°C)

Shoulder Steak

Medium Rare	131°F for 4 to 10 Hours (55.0°C)
Medium	140°F for 4 to 10 Hours (60.0°C)

Sirloin Steak

Medium Rare	131°F for 2 to 10 Hours (55.0°C)
Medium	140°F for 2 to 10 Hours (60.0°C)

Skirt Steak

Medium Rare	131°F for 1 to 2 Days (55.0°C)
Medium	140°F for 1 to 2 Days (60.0°C)

T-Bone Steak

Medium Rare	131°F for 2 to 3 Hours (55.0°C)
Medium	140°F for 2 to 3 Hours (60.0°C)

Tenderloin Steak

Medium Rare	131°F for 2 to 3 Hours (55.0°C)
Medium	140°F for 2 to 3 Hours (60.0°C)

Top Loin Strip Steak

Medium Rare	131°F for 2 to 3 Hours (55.0°C)
Medium	140°F for 2 to 3 Hours (60.0°C)

Top Round Steak

Medium Rare	131°F for 1 to 2 Days (55.0°C)
Medium	140°F for 1 to 2 Days (60.0°C)

Tri-Tip Steak

Medium Rare	131°F for 2 to 10 Hours (55.0°C)
Medium	140°F for 2 to 10 Hours (60.0°C)

CHICKEN AND EGGS

Breast
Rare	136°F for 1 to 4 Hours (57.8°C)
Medium / Typical	140°F - 147°F for 1 to 4 Hours (63.9°C)

Drumstick
Rare	140°F for 90 to 120 Min (60.0°C)
Ideal	148°F - 156°F for 2 to 5 Hours (64.4°C)
For Shredding	160°F - 170°F for 8 to 12 Hours (71.1°C)

Eggs
Over Easy	142°F - 146°F for 45 to 60 Min (62.8°C)
Poached	142°F for 45 to 60 Min (61.1°C)
Perfect	148°F for 45 to 60 Min (64.4°C)
Hard Boiled	149°F - 152°F for 45 to 60 Min (65.6°C)
Pasteurized	135°F for 75 Min (57.2°C)

Leg
Rare	140°F for 90 to 120 Min (60.0°C)
Ideal	148°F - 156°F for 2 to 5 Hours (64.4°C)
For Shredding	160°F - 170°F for 8 to 12 Hours (71.1°C)

Sausage
White Meat	140°F for 1 to 2 Hours (63.9°C)
Mixed Meat	140°F for 90 to 120 Min (60.0°C)

Thigh
Rare	140°F for 90 to 120 Min (60.0°C)
Ideal	148°F - 156°F for 2 to 5 Hours (64.4°C)
For Shredding	160°F - 170°F for 8 to 12 Hours (71.1°C)

Whole Chicken
Rare	140°F for 4 to 6 Hours (60.0°C)
Typical	148°F for 4 to 6 Hours (64.4°C)
Larger	148°F for 6 to 8 Hours (64.4°C)
Butterflied	148°F for 2 to 4 Hours (64.4°C)

DUCK

Breast

Medium-Rare	131°F for 2 to 4 Hours (55.0°C)
Medium	140°F for 2 to 4 Hours (60.0°C)

Drumstick

Medium-Rare	131°F for 3 to 6 Hours (55.0°C)
Well	176°F for 8 to 10 Hours (80.0°C)
Confit	167°F for 10 to 20 Hours (75.0°C)

Foie Gras

Foie Gras	134°F for 35 to 55 Min (56.7°C)

Leg

Medium-Rare	131°F for 3 to 6 Hours (55.0°C)
Well	176°F for 8 to 10 Hours (80.0°C)
Duck Confit	167°F for 10 to 20 Hours (75.0°C)

Sausage

Breast Meat	131°F for 1 to 2 Hours (55.0°C)
Mixed Meat	131°F for 2 to 3 Hours (55.0°C)

Thigh

Medium-Rare	131°F for 3 to 6 Hours (55.0°C)
Well	176°F for 8 to 10 Hours (80.0°C)
Confit	167°F for 10 to 20 Hours (75.0°C)

Whole Duck

Medium-Rare	131°F for 3 to 6 Hours (55.0°C)
Medium	140°F for 3 to 6 Hours (60.0°C)
Confit	167°F for 10 to 20 Hours (75.0°C)

FISH AND SHELLFISH

Arctic Char
"Sushi", Rare	104°F for 10 to 30 Min (40.0°C)
"Sushi", Medium Rare	122°F for 10 to 30 Min (50.0°C)
Medium Rare	132°F for 10 to 30 Min (55.6°C)
Medium	140°F for 10 to 30 Min (60.0°C)

Bass
"Sushi", Rare	104°F for 10 to 30 Min (40.0°C)
"Sushi", Medium Rare	122°F for 10 to 30 Min (50.0°C)
Medium Rare	132°F for 10 to 30 Min (55.6°C)
Medium	140°F for 10 to 30 Min (60.0°C)

Black Sea Bass
"Sushi", Rare	104°F for 10 to 30 Min (40.0°C)
"Sushi", Medium Rare	122°F for 10 to 30 Min (50.0°C)
Medium Rare	132°F for 10 to 30 Min (55.6°C)
Medium	140°F for 10 to 30 Min (60.0°C)

Bluefish
"Sushi", Medium Rare	122°F for 10 to 30 Min (50.0°C)
Medium Rare	132°F for 10 to 30 Min (55.6°C)
Medium	140°F for 10 to 30 Min (60.0°C)

Carp
"Sushi", Medium Rare	122°F for 10 to 30 Min (50.0°C)
Medium Rare	132°F for 10 to 30 Min (55.6°C)
Medium	140°F for 10 to 30 Min (60.0°C)

Catfish
"Sushi", Medium Rare	122°F for 10 to 30 Min (50.0°C)
Medium Rare	132°F for 10 to 30 Min (55.6°C)
Medium	140°F for 10 to 30 Min (60.0°C)

Cod
Rare	104°F for 10 to 30 Min (40.0°C)
"Sushi", Medium Rare	129°F for 10 to 30 Min (53.9°C)
Medium Rare	132°F for 10 to 30 Min (55.6°C)

Flounder
"Sushi", Medium Rare	122°F for 10 to 30 Min (50.0°C)
Medium Rare	132°F for 10 to 30 Min (55.6°C)
Medium	140°F for 10 to 30 Min (60.0°C)

Grouper
"Sushi", Rare	104°F for 10 to 30 Min (40.0°C)
"Sushi", Medium Rare	122°F for 10 to 30 Min (50.0°C)
Medium Rare	132°F for 10 to 30 Min (55.6°C)
Medium	140°F for 10 to 30 Min (60.0°C)

Haddock
"Sushi", Medium Rare	122°F for 10 to 30 Min (50.0°C)
Medium Rare	132°F for 10 to 30 Min (55.6°C)
Medium	140°F for 10 to 30 Min (60.0°C)

Hake
"Sushi", Rare	104°F for 10 to 30 Min (40.0°C)
"Sushi", Medium Rare	122°F for 10 to 30 Min (50.0°C)
Medium Rare	132°F for 10 to 30 Min (55.6°C)
Medium	140°F for 10 to 30 Min (60.0°C)

Halibut
"Sushi", Rare	104°F for 10 to 30 Min (40.0°C)
"Sushi", Medium Rare	129°F for 10 to 30 Min (53.9°C)
Medium Rare	132°F for 10 to 30 Min (55.6°C)
Medium	140°F for 10 to 30 Min (60.0°C)

King Crab Tail
King Crab Tail	140°F for 30 to 45 Min (60.0°C)

Lobster
Medium Rare	126°F for 15 to 40 Min (52.2°C)
Medium	140°F for 15 to 40 Min (60.0°C)

Mackerel
"Sushi", Rare	109°F for 10 to 30 Min (42.8°C)
"Sushi", Medium Rare	122°F for 10 to 30 Min (50.0°C)
Medium Rare	132°F for 10 to 30 Min (55.6°C)

Mahi Mahi

"Sushi", Medium Rare	122°F for 10 to 30 Min (50.0°C)
Medium Rare	132°F for 10 to 30 Min (55.6°C)
Medium	140°F for 10 to 30 Min (60.0°C)

Marlin

"Sushi", Rare	104°F for 10 to 30 Min (40.0°C)
"Sushi", Medium Rare	122°F for 10 to 30 Min (50.0°C)
Medium Rare	132°F for 10 to 30 Min (55.6°C)
Medium	140°F for 10 to 30 Min (60.0°C)

Monkfish

"Sushi", Rare	104°F for 10 to 30 Min (40.0°C)
"Sushi", Medium Rare	118°F for 10 to 30 Min (47.8°C)
Medium Rare	132°F for 10 to 30 Min (55.6°C)
Medium	140°F for 10 to 30 Min (60.0°C)

Octopus

Slow Cook	170°F for 4 to 7 Hours (76.7°C)
Fast Cook	180°F for 2 to 3 Hours (82.2°C)

Red Snapper

"Sushi", Rare	104°F for 10 to 30 Min (40.0°C)
"Sushi", Medium Rare	122°F for 10 to 30 Min (50.0°C)
Medium Rare	132°F for 10 to 30 Min (55.6°C)
Medium	140°F for 10 to 30 Min (60.0°C)

Salmon

"Sushi", Rare	104°F for 10 to 30 Min (40.0°C)
"Sushi", Medium Rare	122°F for 10 to 30 Min (50.0°C)
Medium Rare	132°F for 10 to 30 Min (55.6°C)
Medium	140°F for 10 to 30 Min (60.0°C)

Sardines

"Sushi", Rare	104°F for 10 to 30 Min (40.0°C)
"Sushi", Medium Rare	122°F for 10 to 30 Min (50.0°C)
Medium Rare	132°F for 10 to 30 Min (55.6°C)
Medium	140°F for 10 to 30 Min (60.0°C)

Scallops

Pre-Sear	122°F for 15 to 35 Min (50.0°C)

Scrod

"Sushi", Medium Rare	122°F for 10 to 30 Min (50.0°C)
Medium Rare	132°F for 10 to 30 Min (55.6°C)
Medium	140°F for 10 to 30 Min (60.0°C)

Sea Bass

"Sushi", Rare	104°F for 10 to 30 Min (40.0°C)
"Sushi", Medium Rare	122°F for 10 to 30 Min (50.0°C)
Medium Rare	132°F for 10 to 30 Min (55.6°C)
Medium	140°F for 10 to 30 Min (60.0°C)

Shark

"Sushi", Medium Rare	122°F for 10 to 30 Min (50.0°C)
Medium Rare	132°F for 10 to 30 Min (55.6°C)
Medium	140°F for 10 to 30 Min (60.0°C)

Shrimp

"Sushi" Medium Rare	122°F for 15 to 35 Min (50.0°C)
Medium Rare	132°F for 15 to 35 Min (55.6°C)

Skate

"Sushi", Medium Rare	129°F for 10 to 30 Min (53.9°C)
Medium Rare	132°F for 10 to 30 Min (55.6°C)
Medium	140°F for 10 to 30 Min (60.0°C)

Soft Shell Crab

Standard	145°F for 3 hours (62.8°C)

Sole

"Sushi", Medium Rare	122°F for 10 to 30 Min (50.0°C)
Medium Rare	132°F for 10 to 30 Min (55.6°C)
Medium	143°F for 10 to 30 Min (61.7°C)

Squid

Pre-Sear	113°F for 45 to 60 Min (45.0°C)
Low Heat	138°F for 2 to 4 Hours (58.9°C)
High Heat	180°F for 1 Hour (82.2°C)

Striped Bass

"Sushi", Rare	104°F for 10 to 30 Min (40.0°C)
"Sushi", Medium Rare	122°F for 10 to 30 Min (50.0°C)
Medium Rare	132°F for 10 to 30 Min (55.6°C)
Medium	140°F for 10 to 30 Min (60.0°C)

Sturgeon

"Sushi", Rare	104°F for 10 to 30 Min (40.0°C)
"Sushi", Medium Rare	122°F for 10 to 30 Min (50.0°C)
Medium Rare	132°F for 10 to 30 Min (55.6°C)
Medium	140°F for 10 to 30 Min (60.0°C)

Swordfish

"Sushi", Rare	104°F for 10 to 30 Min (40.0°C)
"Sushi", Medium Rare	122°F for 10 to 30 Min (50.0°C)
Medium Rare	132°F for 10 to 30 Min (55.6°C)
Medium	140°F for 10 to 30 Min (60.0°C)

Tilapia

"Sushi", Rare	104°F for 10 to 30 Min (40.0°C)
"Sushi", Medium Rare	122°F for 10 to 30 Min (50.0°C)
Medium Rare	132°F for 10 to 30 Min (55.6°C)
Medium	140°F for 10 to 30 Min (60.0°C)

Trout

"Sushi", Medium Rare	122°F for 10 to 30 Min (50.0°C)
Medium Rare	132°F for 10 to 30 Min (55.6°C)
Medium	140°F for 10 to 30 Min (60.0°C)

Tuna

"Sushi", Rare	100°F for 10 to 20 Min (37.8°C)
"Sushi", Medium Rare	129°F for 10 to 30 Min (53.9°C)
Medium Rare	132°F for 10 to 30 Min (55.6°C)

Turbot

"Sushi", Medium Rare	129°F for 10 to 30 Min (53.9°C)
Medium Rare	132°F for 10 to 30 Min (55.6°C)
Medium	140°F for 10 to 30 Min (60.0°C)

FRUITS AND VEGETABLES

Acorn Squash	183°F for 1 to 2 Hours (83.9°C)	**Pears**	183°F for 25 to 35 Min (83.9°C)
Apples	183°F for 25 to 40 Min (83.9°C)	**Pineapple**	167°F for 45 to 60 Min (75.0°C)
Artichokes	183°F for 45 to 75 Min (83.9°C)	**Plums**	167°F for 15 to 20 Min (75.0°C)
Asparagus	183°F for 30 to 40 Min (83.9°C)	**Potatoes**	
Banana	183°F for 10 to 15 Min (83.9°C)	Small	183°F for 30 to 60 Min (83.9°C)
		Large	183°F for 60 to 120 Min (83.9°C)
Beet	183°F for 30 to 60 Min (83.9°C)	**Pumpkin**	183°F for 45 to 60 Min (83.9°C)
Broccoli	183°F for 20 to 30 Min (83.9°C)	**Radish**	183°F for 10 to 25 Min (83.9°C)
Brussels Sprouts	183°F for 45 to 60 Min (83.9°C)	**Rhubarb**	141°F for 25 to 45 Min (60.6°C)
Butternut Squash	183°F for 1 to 2 Hours (83.9°C)	**Rutabaga**	183°F for 2 Hours (83.9°C)
Cabbage	183°F for 30 to 45 Min (83.9°C)	**Salsify**	183°F for 45 to 60 Min (83.9°C)
Carrot	183°F for 40 to 60 Min (83.9°C)	**Squash, Summer**	183°F for 30 to 60 Min (83.9°C)
Cauliflower		**Squash, Winter**	183°F for 1 to 2 Hours (83.9°C)
Florets	183°F for 20 to 30 Min (83.9°C)	**Sunchokes**	183°F for 40 to 60 Min (83.9°C)
For Puree	183°F for 2 Hours (83.9°C)		
Stems	183°F for 60 to 75 Min (83.9°C)	**Sweet Potatoes**	
Celery Root	183°F for 60 to 75 Min (83.9°C)	Small	183°F for 45 to 60 Min (83.9°C)
		Large	183°F for 60 to 90 Min (83.9°C)
Chard	183°F for 60 to 75 Min (83.9°C)	**Swiss Chard**	183°F for 60 to 75 Min (83.9°C)
Cherries	183°F for 15 to 25 Min (83.9°C)	**Turnip**	183°F for 30 to 45 Min (83.9°C)
Corn	183°F for 30 to 45 Min (83.9°C)	**Yams**	183°F for 30 to 60 Min (83.9°C)
Eggplant	183°F for 30 to 45 Min (83.9°C)	**Zucchini**	183°F for 30 to 60 Min (83.9°C)
Fennel	183°F for 40 to 60 Min (83.9°C)		
Golden Beets	183°F for 30 to 60 Min (83.9°C)		
Green Beans	183°F for 30 to 45 Min (83.9°C)		
Leek	183°F for 30 to 60 Min (83.9°C)		
Onion	183°F for 35 to 45 Min (83.9°C)		
Parsnip	183°F for 30 to 60 Min (83.9°C)		
Pea Pods	183°F for 30 to 40 Min (83.9°C)		
Peaches	183°F for 30 to 60 Min (83.9°C)		

LAMB

Arm Chop
Medium Rare   131°F for 18 to 36 Hours (55.0°C)
Medium   140°F for 18 to 36 Hours (60.0°C)

Blade Chop
Medium Rare   131°F for 18 to 36 Hours (55.0°C)
Medium   140°F for 18 to 36 Hours (60.0°C)

Breast
Medium-Rare   131°F for 20 to 28 Hours (55.0°C)
Medium   140°F for 20 to 28 Hours (60.0°C)
Well-Traditional 165°F for 20 to 28 Hours (73.9°C)

Leg, Bone In
Rare   126°F for 1 to 2 Days (52.2°C)
Medium Rare   131°F for 2 to 3 Days (55.0°C)
Medium   140°F for 1 to 3 Days (60.0°C)

Leg, Boneless
Medium Rare   131°F for 18 to 36 Hours (55.0°C)
Medium   140°F for 18 to 36 Hours (60.0°C)

Loin Chops
Rare   126°F for 1 to 2 Hours (52.2°C)
Medium Rare   131°F for 2 to 4 Hours (55.0°C)
Medium   140°F for 2 to 3 Hours (60.0°C)

Loin Roast
Rare   126°F for 1 to 2 Hours (52.2°C)
Medium Rare   131°F for 2 to 4 Hours (55.0°C)
Medium   140°F for 2 to 3 Hours (60.0°C)

Loin, Boneless
Rare   126°F for 1 to 2 Hours (52.2°C)
Medium Rare   131°F for 2 to 4 Hours (55.0°C)
Medium   140°F for 2 to 3 Hours (60.0°C)

Neck
Medium Rare   131°F for 2 to 3 Days (55.0°C)
Medium   140°F for 2 to 3 Days (60.0°C)
Well-Traditional 165°F for 1 to 2 Days (73.9°C)

Osso Buco
Medium-Rare   131°F for 1 to 2 Days (55.0°C)
Medium   140°F for 1 to 2 Days (60.0°C)
Well-Traditional 165°F for 1 to 2 Days (73.9°C)

Rack
Rare   126°F for 1 to 2 Hours (52.2°C)
Medium Rare   131°F for 2 to 3 Hours (55.0°C)
Medium   140°F for 1 to 3 Hours (60.0°C)

Rib Chop
Rare   126°F for 1 to 2 Hours (52.2°C)
Medium Rare   131°F for 2 to 3 Hours (55.0°C)
Medium   140°F for 1 to 3 Hours (60.0°C)

Ribs
Medium Rare   131°F for 22 to 26 Hours (55.0°C)
Medium   140°F for 22 to 26 Hours (60.0°C)
Well-Traditional 165°F for 22 to 26 Hours (73.9°C)

Shank
Medium Rare   131°F for 1 to 2 Days (55.0°C)
Medium   140°F for 1 to 2 Days (60.0°C)
Well-Traditional 165°F for 1 to 2 Days (73.9°C)

Shoulder
Medium Rare   131°F for 1 to 2 Days (55.0°C)
Medium   140°F for 1 to 2 Days (60.0°C)
Well-Traditional 165°F for 18 to 36 Hours (73.9°C)

Tenderloin
Rare   126°F for 1 to 2 Hours (52.2°C)
Medium Rare   131°F for 2 to 3 Hours (55.0°C)
Medium   140°F for 1 to 3 Hours (60.0°C)

PORK

Arm Steak

Medium Rare	131°F for 1 to 2 Days	(55.0°C)
Medium	140°F for 1 to 2 Days	(60.0°C)

Baby Back Ribs

Medium Rare	131°F for 8 to 10 Hours	(55.0°C)
Medium	140°F for 8 to 10 Hours	(60.0°C)
Well-Traditional	155°F for 12 to 24 Hours	(68.3°C)

Back Ribs

Medium Rare	131°F for 8 to 12 Hours	(55.0°C)
Medium	140°F for 8 to 12 Hours	(60.0°C)
Well-Traditional	155°F for 12 to 24 Hours	(68.3°C)

Belly

Low and Slow	140°F for 2 to 3 Days	(60.0°C)
In Between	160°F for 18 to 36 Hours	(71.1°C)
High and Fast	180°F for 12 to 18 Hours	(82.2°C)

Blade Chops

Medium Rare	131°F for 8 to 12 Hours	(55.0°C)
Medium	140°F for 8 to 12 Hours	(60.0°C)

Blade Roast

Medium Rare	131°F for 1 to 2 Days	(55.0°C)
Medium	140°F for 1 to 2 Days	(60.0°C)
Well-Traditional	155°F for 1 to 2 Days	(68.3°C)

Blade Steak

Medium Rare	131°F for 18 to 36 Hours	(55.0°C)
Medium	140°F for 18 to 36 Hours	(60.0°C)

Boston Butt

Medium Rare	131°F for 1 to 2 Days	(55.0°C)
Medium	140°F for 1 to 2 Days	(60.0°C)
Well-Traditional	155°F for 1 to 2 Days	(68.3°C)

Butt Roast

Medium Rare	131°F for 18 to 36 Hours	(55.0°C)
Medium	140°F for 18 to 36 Hours	(60.0°C)
Well-Traditional	155°F for 18 to 36 Hours	(68.3°C)

Country Style Ribs

Medium Rare	131°F for 8 to 12 Hours	(55.0°C)
Medium	140°F for 8 to 12 Hours	(60.0°C)
Well-Traditional	155°F for 12 to 24 Hours	(68.3°C)

Fresh Side Pork

Low and Slow	140°F for 2 to 3 Days	(60.0°C)
In Between	160°F for 18 to 36 Hours	(71.1°C)
High and Fast	180°F for 12 to 18 Hours	(82.2°C)

Ground Pork

Medium Rare	131°F for 2 to 4 Hours	(55.0°C)
Medium	140°F for 2 to 4 Hours	(60.0°C)

Ham Roast

Medium Rare	131°F for 10 to 20 Hours	(55.0°C)
Medium	140°F for 10 to 20 Hours	(60.0°C)
Well-Traditional	155°F for 10 to 20 Hours	(68.3°C)

Ham Steak

Medium Rare	131°F for 2 to 3 Hours	(55.0°C)
Medium	140°F for 2 to 3 Hours	(60.0°C)

Kebabs

Medium Rare	131°F for 3 to 8 Hours	(55.0°C)
Medium	140°F for 3 to 8 Hours	(60.0°C)
Well-Traditional	155°F for 3 to 8 Hours	(68.3°C)

Leg (Fresh Ham)

Medium Rare	131°F for 10 to 20 Hours	(55.0°C)
Medium	140°F for 10 to 20 Hours	(60.0°C)
Well-Traditional	155°F for 10 to 20 Hours	(68.3°C)

Loin Chop

Medium Rare	131°F for 3 to 5 Hours	(55.0°C)
Medium	140°F for 2 to 4 Hours	(60.0°C)

Loin Roast

Medium Rare	131°F for 4 to 8 Hours	(55.0°C)
Medium	140°F for 4 to 6 Hours	(60.0°C)

Picnic Roast

Medium Rare	131°F for 1 to 3 Days	(55.0°C)
Medium	140°F for 1 to 3 Days	(60.0°C)
Well-Traditional	155°F for 1 to 3 Days	(68.3°C)

Pork Chops

Medium Rare	131°F for 3 to 6 Hours	(55.0°C)
Medium	140°F for 2 to 4 Hours	(60.0°C)

Rib Chops
Medium Rare   131°F for 5 to 8 Hours (55.0°C)
Medium   140°F for 4 to 7 Hours (60.0°C)

Rib Roast
Medium Rare   131°F for 5 to 8 Hours (55.0°C)
Medium   140°F for 4 to 7 Hours (60.0°C)

Sausage
Medium Rare   131°F for 2 to 3 Hours (55.0°C)
Medium   140°F for 2 to 3 Hours (60.0°C)
Well-Traditional 155°F for 2 to 3 Hours (68.3°C)

Shank
Medium Rare   131°F for 8 to 10 Hours (55.0°C)
Medium   140°F for 8 to 10 Hours (60.0°C)

Shoulder
Medium Rare   135°F for 1 to 2 Days (57.2°C)
Medium   145°F for 1 to 2 Days (62.8°C)
Well-Traditional 155°F for 1 to 2 Days (68.3°C)

Sirloin Chops
Medium Rare   131°F for 6 to 12 Hours (55.0°C)
Medium   140°F for 5 to 10 Hours (60.0°C)

Sirloin Roast
Medium Rare   131°F for 6 to 12 Hours (55.0°C)
Medium   140°F for 5 to 10 Hours (60.0°C)
Well-Traditional 155°F for 10 to 16 Hours (68.3°C)

Spare Ribs
Medium Rare   131°F for 12 to 24 Hours (55.0°C)
Medium   140°F for 12 to 24 Hours (60.0°C)
Well-Traditional 155°F for 12 to 24 Hours (68.3°C)

Spleen
Spleen   145°F for 1 Hour (62.8°C)

Tenderloin
Medium Rare   131°F for 3 to 6 Hours (55.0°C)
Medium   140°F for 2 to 4 Hours (60.0°C)

TURKEY

Breast

"Rare"	136°F for 1 to 4 Hours (57.8°C)
Medium - Typical	147°F for 1 to 4 Hours (63.9°C)

Drumstick

Medium-Rare	140°F for 3 to 4 Hours (60.0°C)
Ideal	148°F for 4 to 8 Hours (64.4°C)
For Shredding	160°F for 18 to 24 Hours (71.1°C)

Leg

Medium-Rare	140°F for 3 to 4 Hours (60.0°C)
Ideal	148°F for 4 to 8 Hours (64.4°C)
For Shredding	160°F for 18 to 24 Hours (71.1°C)

Sausage

White Meat	140°F for 1 to 4 Hours (63.9°C)
Mixed Meat	140°F for 3 to 4 Hours (64.4°C)

Thigh

Medium-Rare	140°F for 3 to 4 Hours (60.0°C)
Ideal	148°F for 4 to 8 Hours (64.4°C)
For Shredding	160°F for 18 to 24 Hours (71.1°C)

FAHRENHEIT TO CELSIUS CONVERSION

This guide gives temperatures in both Fahrenheit and Celsius but to convert from Fahrenheit to Celsius take the temperature, then subtract 32 from it and multiply the result by 5/9:

(Fahrenheit - 32) * 5/9 = Celsius

We've listed out the temperatures from 37°C to 87°C which are the most commonly used range in sous vide.

Celsius	Fahrenheit	Celsius	Fahrenheit
37	98.6	64	147.2
38	100.4	65	149.0
39	102.2	66	150.8
40	104.0	67	152.6
41	105.8	68	154.4
42	107.6	69	156.2
43	109.4	70	158.0
44	111.2	71	159.8
45	113.0	72	161.6
46	114.8	73	163.4
47	116.6	74	165.2
48	118.4	75	167.0
49	120.2	76	168.8
50	122.0	77	170.6
51	123.8	78	172.4
52	125.6	79	174.2
53	127.4	80	176.0
54	129.2	81	177.8
55	131.0	82	179.6
56	132.8	83	181.4
57	134.6	84	183.2
58	136.4	85	185.0
59	138.2	86	186.8
60	140.0	87	188.6
61	141.8	88	190.4
62	143.6	89	192.2
63	145.4	90	194.0

COOKING BY THICKNESS

For more Cooking by thickness information you can view our equipment section on our website where we have an iPhone thickness ruler and free printable thickness cards.

You can find them on our website here:
http://bit.ly/e7Lth2

There are two ways to cook sous vide, one is based on the thickness of the food and the other is based on the desired tenderness.

Cooking based on thickness is how PolyScience, Baldwin, and Nathan started out as they did research on food safety. Cooking sous vide based on thickness basically tells you the minimum time you can cook a piece of meat to ensure it is safe and comes up to temperature in the middle. It doesn't take into account tenderizing time or any other factors. It's often used by restaurants or home cooks who want to minimize cooking time and are using tender cuts of meat that don't need the tenderization.

Cooking sous vide based on tenderness takes into account how tough a piece of meat is and how long it needs to be cooked in order to make it appealing. So a chuck steak needs to be cooked a lot longer than a filet, even though they are both safe after the same amount of time. As long as the minimum cooking time is met for the temperature used, then it's completely safe to eat.

Both sous vide methods have their uses. Thickness-based is great for very tender cuts cooked by people who need them done in the minimum amount of time. Tenderness-based is best for tougher cuts or people that have a range of time that they are interested in.

A Few Notes on the Times

Times were extrapolated from the descriptions in Baldwin's Practical Guide to Sous Vide (http://bit.ly/hGOtjd) and Sous Vide for the Home Cook, as well as Nathan's tables on eGullet and a few other sources. (http://bit.ly/eVHjS3).

The times are also approximate since there are many factors that go into how quickly food is heated. The density of the food matters a lot, which is one reason beef heats differently than chicken. To a lesser degree where you get your beef from will affect the cooking time, and whether the beef was factory raised, farm raised, or grass-fed. Because of this, I normally don't try to pull it out at the exact minute it is done unless I'm in a rush.

The times shown are also minimum times and food can be, and sometimes needs to be, left in for longer periods in order to fully tenderize the meat. If you are cooking food longer, remember that food should not be cooked at temperatures less than 55°C (131°F) for more than 4 hours.

Heat from Refrigerator to Any Temperature

How long it will take to heat an entire piece of meat from 5°C / 41°F to the temperature of the water bath.

Reminder, this food might not be pasteurized at these times and food should not be cooked at temperatures less than 55°C for more than 4 hours.

While there are slight differences in the heating time for different temperatures of water baths, the times usually vary less than 5 to 10% even going from a 44°C bath to a 60.5°C bath, which equates to a difference of 5 minutes every hour. We show the largest value in our chart, so if you are cooking it at a lower temperature you can knock a little of the time off.

Heat from Freezer to Any Temperature

How long it will take to heat an entire piece of meat from -18°C / 32°F to the temperature of the water bath.

Reminder, this food might not be pasteurized at these times and food should not be cooked at temperatures less than 55°C for more than 4 hours.

While there are slight differences in the heating time for different temperatures of water baths, the times usually vary less than 5 to 10% even going from a 44°C bath to a 60.5°C bath, which equates to a difference of 5 minutes every hour. We show the largest value in our chart, so if you are cooking it at a lower temperature you can knock a little of the time off.

Pasteurize from Refrigerator to 55°C / 131°F

This is the amount of time it will take a piece of meat that is 5°C / 41°F to become pasteurized in a 55°C / 131°F waterbath.

Pasteurize from Refrigerator to 60.5°C / 141°F

This is the amount of time it will take a piece of meat that is 5°C / 41°F to become pasteurized in a 60.5°C / 141°F waterbath.

Heat from Refrigerator to Any Temperature

70mm	6h 25m
65mm	5h 30m
60mm	4h 45m
55mm	4h 0m 0s
50mm	3h 15m
45mm	2h 40m
40mm	2h 10m
35mm	1h 40m
30mm	1h 15m 0s
25mm	0h 50m
20mm	0h 35m
15mm	0h 20m
10mm	0h 8m
5mm	0h 2m 0s

Heat from Freezer to Any Temperature

70mm	7 hrs 40 mins
65mm	6 hrs 40 mins
60mm	5 hrs 35 mins
55mm	4 hrs 45 mins
50mm	4 hrs 00 mins
45mm	3 hrs 10 mins
40mm	2 hrs 30 mins
35mm	2 hrs 00 mins
30mm	1 hrs 30 mins
25mm	1 hrs 00 mins
20mm	0 hrs 40 mins
15mm	0 hrs 25 mins
10mm	0 hrs 10 mins
5mm	0 hrs 02 mins

Pasteurize from Refrigerator to 55°C / 131°F

70mm	5 hrs 15 mins
65mm	4 hrs 45 mins
60mm	4 hrs 15 mins
55mm	3 hrs 50 mins
50mm	3 hrs 25 mins
45mm	3 hrs 00 mins
40mm	2 hrs 40 mins
35mm	2 hrs 20 mins
30mm	2 hrs 00 mins
25mm	1 hrs 50 mins
20mm	1 hrs 40 mins
15mm	1 hrs 30 mins
10mm	1 hrs 25 mins
5mm	1 hrs 20 mins

Pasteurize from Refrigerator to 60.5°C / 141°F

70mm	3 hrs 50 mins
65mm	3 hrs 25 mins
60mm	3 hrs 00 mins
55mm	2 hrs 40 mins
50mm	2 hrs 20 mins
45mm	2 hrs 00 mins
40mm	1 hrs 40 mins
35mm	1 hrs 25 mins
30mm	1 hrs 10 mins
25mm	0 hrs 55 mins
20mm	0 hrs 45 mins
15mm	0 hrs 35 mins
10mm	0 hrs 25 mins
5mm	0 hrs 21 mins

Pasteurize from Refrigerator to 57.5°C / 135.5°F

This is the amount of time it will take a piece of chicken that is 5°C / 41°F to become pasteurized in a 57.5°C / 135.5°F waterbath.

Pasteurize from Refrigerator to 60.5°C / 141°F

This is the amount of time it will take a piece of chicken that is 5°C / 41°F to become pasteurized in a 60.5°C / 141°F waterbath.

Pasteurize from Refrigerator to 63.5°C / 146.3°F

This is the amount of time it will take a piece of chicken that is 5°C / 41°F to become pasteurized in a 63.5°C / 146.3°F waterbath.

Pasteurize from Refrigerator to 66°C / 150.8°F

This is the amount of time it will take a piece of chicken that is 5°C / 41°F to become pasteurized in a 66°C / 150.8°F waterbath.

Pasteurize from Refrigerator to 57.5°C / 135.5°F

70mm	6h 30m
65mm	6h
60mm	5h 15m
55mm	4h 45m
50mm	4h 15m
45mm	3h 45m
40mm	3h 20m
35mm	3h
30mm	2h 35m
25mm	2h 20m
20mm	2h 5m
15mm	1h 55m
10mm	1h 45m
5mm	1h 40m

Pasteurize from Refrigerator to 60.5°C / 141°F

70mm	4h 55m
65mm	4h 20m
60mm	3h 50m
55mm	3h 20m
50mm	2h 55m
45mm	2h 30m
40mm	2h 5m
35mm	1h 45m
30mm	1h 25m
25mm	1h 10m
20mm	0h 55m
15mm	0h 45m
10mm	0h 36m
5mm	0h 31m

Pasteurize from Refrigerator to 63.5°C / 146.3°F

70mm	4h 0m 0s
65mm	3h 35m
60mm	3h 10m
55mm	2h 45m
50mm	2h 20m
45mm	2h
40mm	1h 40m
35mm	1h 20m
30mm	1h
25mm	0h 50m
20mm	0h 35m
15mm	0h 23m
10mm	0h 15m
5mm	0h 10m

Pasteurize from Refrigerator to 66°C / 150.8°F

70mm	3h 35m 0s
65mm	3h 10m
60mm	2h 45m
55mm	2h 20m
50mm	2h
45mm	1h 40m
40mm	1h 25m
35mm	1h 5m
30mm	0h 50m
25mm	0h 40m
20mm	0h 26m
15mm	0h 20m
10mm	0h 10m
5mm	0h 5m

Heat Fatty Fish to Any Temperature

These times show how long it will take to heat an entire piece of fatty fish from 5°C / 41°F to any typical temperature.

Reminder, this food might not be pasteurized at these times and food should not be cooked at temperatures less than 55°C / 131°F for more than 4 hours.

While there are slight differences in the heating time for different temperatures of water baths, the times usually vary less than 5 to 10% even going from a 44°C bath to a 60.5°C bath, which equates to a difference of 5 minutes every hour. We show the largest value in our chart, so if you are cooking it at a lower temperature you can knock a little of the time off.

Pasteurize Lean Fish to 55°C / 131°F

This is the amount of time it will take a piece of lean fish that is 5°C / 41°F to become pasteurized in a 55°C / 131°F waterbath.

Pasteurize Lean Fish to 60.5°C / 141°F

This is the amount of time it will take a piece of lean fish that is 5°C / 41°F to become pasteurized in a 60.5°C / 141°F waterbath.

Pasteurize Fatty Fish to 55°C / 131°F

This is the amount of time it will take a piece of fatty fish that is 5°C / 41°F to become pasteurized in a 55°C / 131°F waterbath.

Pasteurize Fatty Fish to 60.5°C / 141°F

This is the amount of time it will take a piece of fatty fish that is 5°C / 41°F to become pasteurized in a 60.5°C / 141°F waterbath.

Heat Fatty Fish to Any Temperature

70mm	6 hrs 25 mins
65mm	5 hrs 30 mins
60mm	4 hrs 45 mins
55mm	4 hrs 00 mins
50mm	3 hrs 15 mins
45mm	2 hrs 40 mins
40mm	2 hrs 10 mins
35mm	1 hrs 40 mins
30mm	1 hrs 15 mins
25mm	0 hrs 50 mins
20mm	0 hrs 35 mins
15mm	0 hrs 20 mins
10mm	0 hrs 08 mins
5mm	0 hrs 02 mins

Pasteurize Lean Fish to 55°C / 131°F

70mm	5 hrs 15 mins
65mm	4 hrs 45 mins
60mm	4 hrs 15 mins
55mm	3 hrs 50 mins
50mm	3 hrs 25 mins
45mm	3 hrs 00 mins
40mm	2 hrs 40 mins
35mm	2 hrs 20 mins
30mm	2 hrs 00 mins
25mm	1 hrs 50 mins
20mm	1 hrs 40 mins
15mm	1 hrs 30 mins
10mm	1 hrs 25 mins
5mm	1 hrs 20 mins

Pasteurize Lean Fish to 60.5°C / 141°F

70mm	6 hrs 30 mins
65mm	6 hrs 00 mins
60mm	5 hrs 15 mins
55mm	4 hrs 45 mins
50mm	4 hrs 15 mins
45mm	3 hrs 45 mins
40mm	3 hrs 20 mins
35mm	3 hrs 00 mins
30mm	2 hrs 35 mins
25mm	2 hrs 20 mins
20mm	2 hrs 05 mins
15mm	1 hrs 55 mins
10mm	1 hrs 45 mins
5mm	1 hrs 40 mins

Pasteurize Fatty Fish to 55°C / 131°F

70mm	5 hrs 15 mins
65mm	4 hrs 45 mins
60mm	4 hrs 15 mins
55mm	3 hrs 50 mins
50mm	3 hrs 25 mins
45mm	3 hrs 00 mins
40mm	2 hrs 40 mins
35mm	2 hrs 20 mins
30mm	2 hrs 00 mins
25mm	1 hrs 50 mins
20mm	1 hrs 40 mins
15mm	1 hrs 30 mins
10mm	1 hrs 25 mins
5mm	1 hrs 20 mins

Pasteurize Fatty Fish to 60.5°C / 141°F

70mm	6 hrs 30 mins
65mm	6 hrs 00 mins
60mm	5 hrs 15 mins
55mm	4 hrs 45 mins
50mm	4 hrs 15 mins
45mm	3 hrs 45 mins
40mm	3 hrs 20 mins
35mm	3 hrs 00 mins
30mm	2 hrs 35 mins
25mm	2 hrs 20 mins
20mm	2 hrs 05 mins
15mm	1 hrs 55 mins
10mm	1 hrs 45 mins
5mm	1 hrs 40 mins

SOUS VIDE RESOURCES

For an up to date look at current books, websites, and other sous vide resources you can visit the list we keep on our website.

You can find it at:
www.cookingsousvide.com/info/sous-vide-resources

Sous vide is a very complex process and there is much more to learn about it besides what has been covered in this book. There is more and more good information available about sous vide cooking. Here are some resources to help you continue to learn more.

BOOKS

Under Pressure
By Thomas Keller

This book shows you the extent of what is possible through sous vide cooking. The recipes aren't easy, and they require a lot of work but they can provide great inspiration for dishes of your own. If you are interested in expanding your concept of what can be accomplished through cooking then this is a must have.

Cooking for Geeks
By Jeff Potter

If you are interested in the Geekier aspects of cooking then this book does a great job. It takes you through the basics of setting up your kitchen all the way up to kitchen hacks and sous vide cooking.

On Food and Cooking
By Harold McGee

This is the ultimate guide to the scientific aspects of cooking. If you like to know why things happen in the kitchen, at every level, you'll find this book fascinating.

Beginning Sous Vide: Low Temperature Recipes and Techniques for Getting Started at Home
By Jason Logsdon

Our main book covering sous vide. It deals a lot with the various equipment options and has over 100 recipes, some of which have been adapted for grilling specifically for this book.

Cooking Sous Vide: A Guide for the Home Cook
By Jason Logsdon

My first book and the first book written exclusively for the home cook learning sous vide. Most of the information from it has been updated and adapted for inclusion in Beginning Sous Vide.

Sous-Vide Cuisine
By Joan Roca

From the authors: "we propose our book, as a progression that involves three concepts of sous-vide: Storage, Cooking and Cuisine." Be sure to get a copy that is in English, as many copies are not.

Modernist Cuisine: The Art and Science of Cooking

By Nathan Myhrvold

This just released and aims to be the bible of modernist cuisine. It's over 2,400 pages costs $500 and was several years in the making. If you are serious about learning the newly developing modernist techniques then this might be worth the investment.

Sous Vide for the Home Cook

By Douglas Baldwin

Baldwin helped to define and codify home sous vide cooking with his free online guide. His book is a nice intro to the subject, including food safety, and has many simple recipes to follow.

Sous Vide

By Viktor Stampfer

A collection of some of Viktor's best sous vide recipes. Be sure to get a copy that is in English, as many copies are not.

WEBSITES

Cooking Sous Vide

http://www.cookingsousvide.com

This is the main website where I contribute sous vide articles. We update it regularly with original recipes and news from around the sous vide community. There are also community features such as forums and question and answer pages.

SVKitchen

http://www.svkitchen.com

A very nice site on sous vide cooking. They touch on everything from standard sous vide swordfish to making your own preserved lemons with sous vide.

Sous Vide: Recipes, Techniques & Equipment

http://forums.egullet.org/index.php?showtopic=116617&st=0

A very long forum string from eGullet, about 98 pages long at this time that covers almost everything you need to know about sous vide if you have the time to look through it all. I suggest starting near the end and working towards the front.

APPS

We 2 apps for the iPhone and iPad app available, as well as one for the Android. You can search in the app store for "Sous Vide" and ours should be near the top, published by "Primolicious".

Papers and Research

USDA Guide

http://www.fsis.usda.gov/OPPDE/rdad/FSISNotices/RTE_Poultry_Tables.pdf

The US government guide to poultry and beef cooking times.

Practical Guide to Sous Vide

http://amath.colorado.edu/~baldwind/sous-vide.html

Written by Douglas Baldwin, this is one of the best guides available for the scientific principles behind sous vide cooking and a pioneering work in home sous vide cooking.

Sous Vide Safety

http://www.seriouseats.com/2010/04/sous-vide-basics-low-temperature-chicken.html

A nice look at the basics of low temperature cooking, specifically as it applies to chicken.

PHOTO CREDITS

Converting Existing Recipes: http://www.flickr.com/photos/ginnerobot

Sous Vide and Grilling Tips: http://www.flickr.com/photos/katerha

Hamburger and Sandwiches: http://www.flickr.com/photos/chichacha

Kebabs: http://www.flickr.com/photos/dnorman

Sausages and Hotdogs: http://www.flickr.com/photos/stuart_spivack

Classic BBQ: http://www.flickr.com/photos/paulk

Salads: http://www.flickr.com/photos/veganfeast/

Steak: http://www.flickr.com/photos/gudlyf

Chicken: http://www.flickr.com/photos/jar0d

Fish: http://www.flickr.com/photos/avlxyz

Lamb: http://www.flickr.com/photos/hmk

Pork: http://www.flickr.com/photos/mccun934

Party Foods: http://www.flickr.com/photos/norrisc

Time and Temperature Charts: http://www.flickr.com/photos/besighyawn

Made in the USA
Middletown, DE
01 April 2016